For
Cornelius Murphy,

Sincerest Best Wishes

BANKRUPT

**A Society
Living in the Future**

BANKRUPT

A Society
Living in the Future

James V. McTevia

Foreword by M. Scott Peck, M.D.

Momentum Books Ltd.
Ann Arbor

© 1992 by James V. McTevia

Manufactured in the United States of America

1995   1994   1993   1992   5   4   3   2   1

Dust jacket design by Tom Roy

Published by Momentum Books Ltd.
210 Collingwood, Suite 106
Ann Arbor, Michigan 48103
USA

ISBN 1-879094-18-5

Library of Congress Cataloging-in-Publication Data

McTevia, James V., 1936–
    Bankrupt : a society living in the future / James V. McTevia ;
foreword by M. Scott Peck.
    p.   cm.
    ISBN 1-879094-18-5 (hardcover) : $21.95
    1. Debt—United States. 2. Finance, Personal—United States.
3. Corporate debt—United States. 4. Debts, Public—United States.
I. Title.
HG3711.U6M39   1992
332.7′5′0973—dc20   92-27533
                                                              CIP

Contents

Foreword

As a psychiatrist, I am a relatively well certified and trained expert on the subject of sanity or mental health. We psychiatrists are able to deal with issues of insanity and people with mental illnesses only insofar as we have some definition or understanding of mental health and sanity.

I write this foreword because here is a book about sanity.

When I was still in the private practice of psychiatry, I could not function unless my patients paid me. Consequently, they and I had a serious problem when early in the course of our work together—as not infrequently happened—their checks would bounce. I then essentially had only two alternatives. One was to refuse to see a client anymore, often referring his bill to a collection agency. The other alternative was to practice what I came to call "checkbook therapy." I would ask patients to bring in their checkbooks to see how they balanced them. It is amazing how many seemingly sane, relatively well put together human beings, not diagnosable as schizophrenic, biochemically deranged, or otherwise severely mentally ill, balance their checkbooks! But only when they learned to do so could their therapy proceed.

This book teaches individuals what they used to have to pay me a hundred dollars an hour for ... often hour after hour. It is a mental health bargain for an enormous number of men and women who need to absorb the simple principles of fiscal sanity. It will also be a bargain if they pass it on to their children.

That is one reason I have written this foreword. The other is because for almost 30 years I have routinely doubted my own sanity. For during that time, I have been a citizen of a nation that has consistently refused to balance its checkbook.

There was once a long tradition of our federal government maintaining a level of debt approximately equal to its annual budget or income. From 1938 until 1945 our government openly deviated from this policy by virtue of the publicly declared crisis of World War II. By the end of the war, our national debt stood at twice our annual budget. Nonetheless, despite the Marshall Plan and the Korean War, we managed to pay off our excess debt with the result that by 1955 the national debt once again was equal to the federal government's income. And there, in accord with sound tradition, the level stood for the next decade.

But in 1966 something bizarre began to happen. Without any publicly announced crisis, our government began once again to go into serious debt. Silently. Almost secretly. And continued. And continued. Since that time, our national debt—adjusted for inflation—has increased over 250 percent and currently stands at over $3^{1}/_{2}$ times our annual budget. And is still increasing. No one even seems to think that we can pay it back anymore. Indeed, the practice of increasing debt has become normative—normal. We crazily think it to be "healthy," as if this "fly now, pay later" approach to life was somehow perfectly reasonable.

As a psychiatrist, I am seriously concerned about the health of our nation when it cannot even balance its checkbook—the very beginning of a healing process.

There are a number, like myself, who have screamed that we are "mortgaging our children's futures." We only seem malcontents and doomsayers. Meanwhile, Americans obsess about the effects of sexual pornography upon children. Yet we seem to have amazingly little concern about the effect of our unbalanced budget, not only upon our children's fiscal future but upon their minds. What message are we giving them? Going into ever greater debt, year after year after year, for no apparent reason, is what our leaders declare to be the norm. It is the practice. It is the way things are done. Think of the effect of *this* pornography!

Our federal government is bankrupt. It is fiscally bankrupt

and spiritually bankrupt. Indeed, it has become fiscally bankrupt precisely because it has been spiritually bankrupt these many years.

Perhaps other clear books have been written on this subject, but I haven't seen them. Finally, *finally*, someone has come along—an ordinary person, someone who never even went to college—to finally proclaim that the emperor has no clothes.

Thank God. Jim McTevia has helped me to no longer doubt my sanity. Rather, he very simply puts before us what I have come to call "the holiness of numbers."

This is a sane book about sanity. Please read it. Perhaps weep, and then scream out in rage about what our leaders are doing to us.

M. Scott Peck, M.D.

To Joni:

You have made my little world a Shangri-La.

Introduction

For more than 30 years I have been a box-seat spectator at a game called Living in the Future. The players always end up in trouble. Far too often, for serious players, there is tragedy.

Nonetheless, Living in the Future is the most popular game in town.

Individuals play it. Corporations play it. Governments play it.

Day laborers, waitresses, Harvard Law grads and CEOs all shuffle the deck and ante up with zeal.

Though the rules are quite clear, the players suffer genuine shock when their chips begin to disappear. Denial, in fact, is usually a good sign that the final round is at hand.

That's when the players discover that nothing—except perhaps the loss of a loved one—corrodes, encircles and finally overwhelms the spirit like Living in the Future.

I have seen six players take their own lives.

In my youth, at games where the ante was small, I saw agony and shame on the faces of couples who were losing nothing more than their bedroom furniture. Their world may not have been much, but they thought it was theirs. Then it was hauled out the door.

Later, and on a grander scale, I would encounter the sometimes bewildered, sometimes angry, sometimes blank faces of companies' entire work forces as they learned that they, and their families, no longer had a livelihood.

These are not imaginary faces drawn by some econometric software. The agony, the bewilderment, the anger, the tears, the shouting and the stifling silences are real. I know, because often I have been the one who had to stand up and deliver the news.

We are talking about rampant *debt*. Debt that is amassed in ill-thought, unrealistic and—more often than you would ever imagine—unbelievable ratio to ability to pay.

Unrealistic debt is what makes Living in the Future possible, for whatever period of time the game may last.

Clearly, I am a radical on the subject. Three decades of seeing the carnage first-hand will give you that perspective.

I suppose, for example, that a narcotics officer would define the most serious of our society's numerous problems in terms of cocaine and heroin.

He may be right, of course. When the menu of ills is so extensive, and the portions so large, it's difficult to prioritize. I came to adulthood in the '50s—when drugs were mostly of the "miracle" variety, morals were straighter than a Kansas highway, the gap between haves and have-nots seemed to be shrinking instead of growing, we all loved Lucy and liked Ike, and 20 percent was more likely to be the amount you *financed* on a car than the amount you paid down. Like the song says, times were simple then. And I must admit I liked the way we were.

We all carry our own baggage through life, and that legacy of having shaped my values in the good, gray '50s is probably my biggest suitcase. I suspect that in many quarters I have been perceived as the good, gray McTevia, waltzing through the go-go years and the trying-to-go-go years with an inordinately wary view of this beast called credit—though a good hand to call upon when a situation went sour. I also suspect that as the '90s run their course, a very large number of individuals and companies will wish they had taken a prudently gray point of view.

The credit beast, in fact, has been allowed to roam so far out of its cage that I would respectfully be forced to argue with my narcotics officer friend as to whether dope or debt is the greater evil at large in the land. I have seen at least a big chunk of the future, and it is *debt service*. Or, as a frequent alternative, unserviced debt. The consequences of either are not pretty.

When it comes to debt, everyone is a user. No substance is *ab*used by so many. The average house is home to several credit junkies. Even our corporations consume mind-altering doses of the stuff. Our government is snorting by far the biggest line of credit ever known to man, so strongly addicted that its most forgiving friends—who once looked the other way—are finally whispering about the problem.

Our government, in fact, is living so far into the future that its debt surpasses mere unbelievability. The federal deficit— your debt and mine, and for generations of descendants to come if payment is in fact to be made just on the *interest*—is inconceivable. My profession involves looking at a troubled company's debt and deciding what to do about it. I do know how to read a balance sheet. But I readily confess that even I cannot comprehend all those zeroes being rung up on Washington's meter. It's not a number. It's a way of life.

On the other hand, I'm not an economist. And I'm sure at least one of them is available to explain every conceivable crunching of that inconceivable number.

Nor am I a sociologist or a political scientist offering a textbook for solving all the nation's ills. I don't have the requisite diplomas on the wall to venture seriously down that path. In a brief section at the end of this book, I do offer a *starting point*. The intervening pages will, I hope, help you to share my absolute conviction of where that starting point lies.

What most of these pages offer is well-credentialed common sense and a good deal of practical experience, which I hope will help you or your business solve *your* financial crisis—or, better yet if it is not too late, chart a course to avoid one.

You will not find a total blueprint for success here, no one-stop self-help volume. I would gladly pass that gold ring on to you if I possessed it. Whatever it is that you do to make a living, whatever product you make or service you offer, is something you already do far, far better than I—or any financial consultant—ever could. That simple, very positive part of the picture is something that often gets lost in the morass of a serious setback. If you've had success in the past, it is only because of *your* expertise and labor that there is *anything* to fine-tune, or reorganize, or salvage, or even to liquidate.

What I can do with confidence is illuminate the crucial elements of *sound financial strategy*. That applies to any person, couple, small business, large business—or even, I like to think, any government. Ambulance drivers don't need exhaustive corroborative research to tell you all about the effects of alcohol on the highway. And after arriving at the scenes of hundreds of financial disasters, I think it's safe to report that certain behavioral patterns are generally revealed in the wreckage.

If your personal or business financial affairs are already in trouble because of poor financial strategy, I can share the principles that have helped my company put scores of organizations, from manufacturers to hospitals, back on track. If the situation is beyond turnaround, you should know that losing the game is not a matter of turning off the phones and walking away. There *are* strategies to minimize the loss and the pain for you, your creditors and your employees.

Details will emerge as we go on. But if you are seriously near financial collapse, or if you are on course to reach that point, there are some facts you must comprehend immediately.

This is *not* the worst thing that could happen to you. Even if you lose a house, or a car, or both. Even if you wind up in bankruptcy. Even if you lose a company that you, and maybe your father and your grandfather, worked years to nurture. Life is far, far more than this persona that you are right now defining by your net worth, or by some buildings and equipment, or by some very expensive sheet metal you are using for transportation. Trust me. I have seen scores of clients learn this fact, survive and prosper.

The embarrassment of it all? Of course. Acute, often internalized, embarrassment is the one constant in all these sad situations. Often it is the reason that a business principal waits so long to seek outside help that it is too late to do a proper job. Embarrassment is not a strong enough word. The emotion is so intense that you come to believe you are alone in this morass, that *no one else* has managed to get himself in such a sorry situation. But thousands and thousands have preceded you, of course; and thousands are waiting in line.

Above all else, you must understand that without exception —save an act of God or your state lottery commission—your financial crisis will not go away if you do not act. It will grow, until you cannot address it, let alone resolve it. The self-satisfaction and esteem that you will reap from confronting your problems is greater than any financial loss imaginable.

Some of the things I'm going to tell you in these pages are things you *should* already know. Events in the real world suggest, however, that these are lessons ill-taught. So much so that, as the kids were still saying the last time I looked, it's awesome.

Most likely it is not rote knowledge, but *understanding,* that is in short supply. Or perhaps it is simply a lack of *resolve.* I hope this book fills in enough blanks, supplies enough examples, brings enough dry truisms to life, and reveals enough of the human element behind the balance sheet to spark a little more understanding and resolve.

If I can spare just a few readers the pain that ultimately accompanies Living in the Future, I'll be happy.

PART ONE

Finding My Way

1

Tomorrow Is *Another* Day

She was a blonde and blue-eyed goddess, a neighbor's cousin. I fell in love with her at first sight. I was 12, and about to encounter my first personal financial crisis.

All the elements of real-world adult financial crises would be manifested in and around the Mariner Theatre in Marine City, Michigan, that summer day in 1948. I wish I could say that from that day forward I balanced my personal books, avoided overextension, and led my financial life in the present rather than the future, culminating in a career as a financial and management consultant. That would make an engaging fable, but it would be far from the truth.

The story of the Blonde Goddess is worth retelling anyway.

For one thing, I do indeed remember her; but I remember the financial details even more vividly. If that doesn't say something about the importance of our subject matter, nothing will.

For another thing, it is amazing how byzantine a mess I concocted in an age, figuratively and literally, of innocence. When you are determined to live in the future, beyond your means, sometimes only a slow wit can save you from disaster.

And finally, it is absolutely uncanny how the emotions, the traps, the frenzied and futile efforts to improvise a quick fix so closely parallel adult scenarios running several million dollars deeper into the hole.

Had Carolann not been coy, the whole episode would not have unfolded. But something about Carolann's approach/avoid manner during her weekend visits to the neighbors made it clear that she recognized qualities in me that the local girls did not.

When she agreed to go to the movies with me, however, it may not have been because of any such qualities. More likely it was my declaration of financial independence. Specifically, I said I would buy tickets for her, for me and for several friends— as well as footing the bill for snacks in the theater and a trip to the next-door ice cream parlor after the show.

On paper, this would fly. My mother had negotiated several lucrative lawnmowing contracts for me. Unfortunately, as the Great Day neared, Marine City had not seen any rain for a month. I began to panic, lost my appetite, had trouble sleeping. My total focus was directed at raising cash to avoid looking the fool.

I borrowed whatever money I could from several friends. Still not enough.

I negotiated several advance payments on mowing jobs to be done when, one assumed, the rains would finally arrive. To carry off this ploy, I offered substantial discounts—which I learned later were probably unnecessary.

On the morning of the Great Day, I was mortgaged to the hilt, buried in debt, facing a future of working for nothing—and I felt absolutely terrific. The Blonde Goddess and I were going to the show!

Actually, it was the Blonde Goddess, myself, three other girls and three other boys. Multiply each unit of cost by eight.

When we arrived, the marquee boldly proclaimed: "Double Feature." And the little card in the cashier's window revealed that I had substantially miscalculated the tab.

What followed was a panic-state blur of fuzzy thinking. I sent the girls in ahead, on grounds I had to make seating arrangements at the ice cream parlor. Then I cut a deal with one of the boys, buying him a ticket and giving him the rest of the money to buy snacks for the girls. He was then to execute an old ploy we had used many times—letting the rest of us boys inside from an alley emergency exit.

I was in the alley for an hour before accepting the fact that my improvisation was dead in the water. My other two friends packed it in and left much earlier, after directing considerable ridicule and scorn my way. I learned later that the theater manager had taken a seat directly opposite the alley exit.

My confederate on the inside followed instructions perfectly. He spent every last cent on snacks for the girls, who were suitably impressed. The Blonde Goddess, in fact, fell madly in love with my friend the sugar daddy.

So I heard, at least. I never saw Carolann face-to-face again, by design. I was too embarrassed.

Meanwhile, I worked hard for a month and a half, often for free, while paying off my debts. If you had asked me at the time, I would have told you I was "broke." There were many miles to go before I would have used the proper term. I was a walking definition of "insolvency." And a victim of Living in the Future.

* * *

Forty-two years later, as the country completed a decade-long orgy of Living in the Future, I warned clients and anyone who cared to listen that serious troubles lay ahead.

This did not require genius, or a crystal ball. In the '80s, virtually everyone and every institution—from the Congress to the smallest business, from Michael Milken to the blue-collar guy next door—was out in that theater alley trying to leverage a cozy afternoon with the Blonde Goddess. Anyone with a modicum of real-world experience could see that an awful lot of lawns would be mowed for free in the '90s.

The word "leverage" itself came into currency in the '80s, as if jargon could obscure the avalanche of unrealistic debt pouring through Wall Street's canyons and Everytown's quiet, heavily mortgaged side streets. Consumer debt more than doubled. Corporate debt more than doubled. The national debt, never to be outdone, *tripled*.

My Merriam-Webster *New Collegiate Dictionary* defines leverage as "the use of credit to enhance one's *speculative* capacity (buying stocks on margin is a form of leverage)." Those are my italics on "speculative." In other words, "lever," as in "one-armed bandit," as in using whichever piece of unmaximized plastic you may possess to make a run at Las Vegas. You may come to the table with nothing, but by anteing up the future you can pull that lever to your heart's content.

Why? What is the common thread among all these lever-agers, be they Italian-suited financiers shuffling junk bonds or bejeaned teenagers charging a sack of heavy metal audio tapes at the discount store?

In truth, as we will see, many threads interconnect Living in the Future players of any stripe. But the simple (and best) answer is this: *"A person who lives in the future possesses un-wavering, unfounded, blind faith that tomorrow will be better than today."* As surely as I knew it would rain on those lawns in Marine City, these players go to sleep confident of—or at least counting on—a better tomorrow. Players who are well aware that today's receivables may be as soft as brie at a July picnic will, nonetheless and incredibly, spend against *tomorrow's* yet-unmade promises to pay.

One measure of American life has indeed been that *most* tomorrows have been better than *most* todays. Progress—material progress, at least—historically has been our economy's most frequent product. We are accustomed to seeing our standard of living, which is measured solely in material terms, on the rise. Numerous negative blips have soiled the progress chart, of course. And those who lived through the Great Depression would have considerable difficulty hearing it described as a "blip." But in the '80s we financed our personal, corporate and governmental lives as if even minor blips were extinct, as if an exponentially increasing standard of living somehow had become a birthright.

Could anyone possibly have believed that to be true? Not being a novelist, or even a sociologist, I can't comment on fanciful explanations. For example, if someone were to suggest that a national death wish was afoot in the '80s, or that some Eve of Destruction malaise had us all voting "tomorrow be damned" with our plastic—then I would have to withdraw from the conversation. Too speculative. And I'm not an economist, so I cannot comment meaningfully on any analysis suggesting that the hard times actually arrived a dozen years ago, and that we staved off the consequences by borrowing our lungs out. Too theoretical.

I'm just a numbers man with a simple vision of reality, based on real-world experience. Let the novelists and politicians and economists and other creative types flesh it out with high drama. But I *know* the key text of this morality play, the fount from which all subtexts flow, because I have seen it in a professional capacity every day of my adult life. We got where we are—in the tank, to use the vernacular—by Living in the Future.

That has been the kernel problem with virtually every financially troubled company or individual I have counseled over the years. By the '80s, however, Living in the Future became a game played not just by the few and the soon-to-be troubled, but a national pastime as common as color TV. America, having grown accustomed to progressively larger toys and more and more of them, got greedy beyond belief and sold its children and its children's children down the river just to keep the toy shelf full for this generation. I know in my heart, in my mind and in a warehouse full of case files that it is all as simple as that.

How inconvenient that this credit orgy should have commenced on the eve of an era when, by popular consensus, the next American generation will be the first to live not as "well" as their parents.

How thoughtless of tomorrow to reveal itself as not only no better than today, but as a step *away* from the materialist heaven we all had in mind.

How annoying that, therefore, the debt we couldn't afford yesterday will be even more difficult—if not impossible—to pay off today.

How embarrassing that the people of the greatest nation in the world, as we are accustomed to seeing ourselves, turn out to be—individually and jointly—bankrupt.

Harsh? I don't think so. If you wish to quarrel with that

assessment, please answer one question: Who is going to pay the bill? Us or our children?

And then, since it is considered bad manners to raise a problem without offering a solution, please answer one more question—because the simple answer to this one is the first step to *any* solution, mine or yours or the politicians': When will the meter finally stop running? When will our society finally screw up the courage to get out the scissors, cut up all of its plastic, and stop spending resources it lacks but *assumes* will be there tomorrow?

That is merely a first step. But it is the *only* first step. It is the sole intelligent action when confronted with the knowledge that tomorrow might not be better than today, and in fact might be a hell of a lot worse.

Maybe it's the simplicity of it all that is so befuddling. I don't know why. After all, if someone is bleeding to death, any nearby Boy Scout will know enough to step forward and apply a tourniquet.

Maybe it only seems so simple because of the places I've been and the things I've seen. It certainly took much more than the Blonde Goddess to make me understand.

My consulting firm maintains a justifiably high reputation in every facet of the commercial and legal universe in which troubled companies and individuals find themselves struggling to survive: banks, creditors, accounting firms, the courts. I can lay legitimate claim, in fact, to having invented the profession of "turnaround specialist," a field whose directory now runs to several hundred pages. I lecture, I write articles, the news media often interview me. And someday, I suppose, some business school will offer a master's degree in turnaround management.

I never spent a day in college, however. Whatever depth of understanding I may have of financial crises, from the balance sheet to the emotional toll, is a result of having worn virtually every hat in the credit industry—beginning at the lowest imaginable level. That, and a few financial crises that I have myself endured, have been worth more to me on the job than any formal education I might have pursued.

In fact, if any of this narrative begins to touch a nerve, if you recognize yourself Living in the Future, it may be some consolation to know that I am a spendthrift. If I have some loose cash, I must bury it somewhere or it's gone. At times in my life I have lived far into the future. And even though I have conquered the credit beast, at least by late 20th-Century American standards, I remain in awe of my willingness to make a down payment on one of the few things that are not for sale—the future.

When I first thought of writing a book, I'm not sure I envisioned talking about my spendthrift nature or about 12-year-old Blonde Goddesses. I think I expected to begin at the top of page one as James V. McTevia, Management and Adjustment Consultant, and proceed to share as much of that high-priced advice as is possible between the covers of a book.

That is indeed my goal. But when I picked up a pen, my very first image was of that intense humiliation outside the Mariner Theatre. So very trivial. So very many years ago. Yet so unforgettable. All financial problems, to an outsider or an academic, appear as nothing more than a dispassionate series of numbers recorded in neat columns. But when it is *your* marriage, or *your* factory, or *your* job that is in harm's way—then you realize what an emotional, human equation is on the table.

I like to think that in my professional practice I pay extraordinary attention to the human element of the equation. That dimension of my practice found its roots long before I hung up a shingle and created my current professional world. To fully understand the view from that vantage point, you must share some of the experiences that led me there.

That is why Part One talks of Blonde Goddesses, and of the woman who hit me with a broom.

2

Born to Spend?

As a kid, I never knew how much money my father made. I'm not sure it ever occurred to me to ask. If I had asked, and if he had told me, I'm not sure the number would have meant anything to me.

I did know and understand three important things.

First, Dad had an office job at an auto plant.

Second, we lived in a nice house where we were never hungry, never cold, never wanting for any of the basics of life.

Third, if I wanted anything else, I was to go out and earn money to pay for it.

At an early age I discovered that I liked having money to spend, so I mowed lawns and cleaned floors at the sweet shop.

In retrospect, this was one of my family's great gifts to me: letting me know that work produced money, and suggesting that not working did not produce money. Like many important truths, it is blessedly simple. But far too many kids—often those who live in houses where money is plentiful—never learn.

Sadly, it cannot be said that I learned anything at all in my youth about thrift—and certainly nothing about the perils of Living in the Future. Maybe that's because my parents never strayed into unrealistic debt and assumed that no one else would, either. I do know that my parents would be appalled at the debt service they would be *expected* to carry today. And that my grandparents quite simply would not have believed it. Such has been the credit curve as each succeeding generation robs from tomorrow to make sure the toy shelf gets ever larger and ever more full of trifles.

My hometown, Marine City, is a community of 5,000 on the St. Clair River, which flows south about 50 miles from Lake Huron to Lake St. Clair. The riverbank slopes gently downward from Water Street, the main drag, and from anywhere in town you can see Canada three-quarters of a mile across the water.

Nothing moves along the world's greatest inland seaway without traversing the St. Clair River. Any restaurant or pub along the river is a superb vantage point to watch a steady stream of lake boats hauling massive tonnages of every commodity imaginable. Visitors from afar are usually stunned at the size of these "boats," which is the proper term, though many of them would dwarf the average oceangoing ship. The waves generated by a North Atlantic gale would snap a 1,000-foot lake monster in half. And sometimes, particularly in November when the inland sea assumes its most wrathful cast, that is exactly what happens.

So my hometown was aptly named. It was a mariner's place, all right, providing many crewmen—including skippers and chief engineers—for the boats. Three of my uncles sailed the lakes, and a close family friend, George Vargo, covered lakes shipping for years as a writer for the Benton Harbor Herald-Palladium. That was enough of a connection to get me a summer job as a coal passer on the Mataffa when I was a ninth-grader, and to keep me afloat literally and financially through my teen-aged years.

I was already becoming a *cash* junkie. I did not live in the future, but I extracted every possible penny from the present. Which is where I left it all, as quickly as possible. That is a consumerist feat—being in high school, sailing the lakes, and soon broke. I achieved this despite working in a dry cleaners while I was ashore during the school year. As soon as I could get a driver's license, I bought a 1948 Plymouth coupe. Shortly afterward I wrecked it. Totaled it. On the other hand, I don't recall any Blonde Goddess financial episodes in that period. It was all cash going down the tubes.

The nuns at Holy Cross High must have had a tolerant streak, because eventually they granted me a diploma with the class of '54. I'm not sure why. I was mischievous, continually in some kind of minor trouble, and my father often had to visit the school to discuss my behavior. Years later, when one of my first newspaper commentaries was published, I got a call from the nun who taught me in fifth grade. Her comment was along the lines of, "I believe in the power of prayer. But this, James, is difficult to believe."

By the time I had a high school diploma I was already a seasoned sailor, of sorts, and there was no question about my next step—onto the boats full-time. You must understand, this was a *very* good job. I'm sure I made considerably more money than my father, almost immediately.

I worked my way upward—from coal handler to fireman to oiler. The food was first-class, the pay kept getting better and, it was always said, "You can't spend it on the lakes." No hurdle was too high for my spending habits, however. I could disappear for 15 days in an engine room and then, in a quick visit to shore, find a way to unload my accumulated liquid assets. In retrospect, even older and wiser and totally cognizant of my predilection for dumping cash on any handy barrelhead, I find this to be an incredible performance.

Somewhere after high school, with even more money rolling into my wallet, I discovered that by tapping the future here and there I could spend at a more furious pace. There was a Chrysler that itself seemed to extend the breadth and length of an ore carrier. I wasn't exactly a careful budgeteer at the time, so I cannot recall all the specifics. But I know that by 1957 I was thoroughly acquainted with the phenomenon of mail that arrived in business envelopes and went into an ominous pile, awaiting action.

In January of '57 I met a girl from Port Huron, where the

St. Clair begins its journey from Lake Huron down toward Detroit. By April Joan and I were engaged and by September we were married. To this union we brought ourselves and not much else. Our savings were zero, zilch, absolutely nothing. We both had bills to pay, despite the fact that I was working one of the best middle-class blue-collar jobs in the Midwest.

I pulled enough cash together to pay for a ring and for the first month's rent on an apartment. Joan didn't think young lovers should be separated for nine or 10 months of the year, and neither did I. So it was goodby boats, hello shore, wonder what I'll do for a living?

I suppose youth has to be listed as both an asset and a debit in any accounting of our situation, because I was too inexperienced to understand fully just what a mess we were in. On the one hand, you do dumb things; on the other hand, you have resilience and energy and a sense of immortality. With a little luck you can channel those qualities onto a path that will lead to more solid ground.

Was I really a born spender? Well, of course not. I *learned* that questionable skill at an early age. It was honest spending, at least, because it was my money and it was in my hand. But soon I joined the vanguard of the Living in the Future crowd, post-war children of parents who knew better but couldn't imagine the credit binge that lay ahead. So I don't really fault them for not teaching me the perils of Living in the Future. I do fault any modern parents who fail to make a serious effort to pass this knowledge to their children. Chances are any parent today need look no further than his own financial situation to understand just how imperative this lesson is.

What I did have from my upbringing, what saved Joan and me, and what by a total accident of time and place took me onward to a rewarding career, was that strong appetite for work. Show me a legal and honest activity that produced cash, and I was ready and eager to go. Those of you who remember the late '50s around Detroit, however, will recall that ready and eager were in line applying for jobs on every block.

So our married life began with not a penny left from a brief but lucrative career as a sailor, with bills beginning to pile up on the shelf, and with the breadwinner unemployed.

I took a job selling subscriptions to the *St. Anthony Messenger* door-to-door, and kept looking for something better.

3

Life at the Bottom

If you looked at my resume and saw that my first real job ashore was with a finance company, you might say, "Well, that makes sense. McTevia always had an affinity for handling money."

As a reader of this book, you already know better. The finance company, which shall remain anonymous in these pages, was just a job at a place where a friend worked. I certainly had demonstrated no aptitude for either cash or credit matters. If my friend had worked at Joe's Garage, I might be struggling today with the complexities of trying to tune an engine that contains more computers than gaskets.

Instead, I started right out struggling with the complexities—mostly moral and emotional—of processing loans for low-income people who shouldn't have been borrowing the cash in the first place. I also collected from customers who fell behind on payments. And, in my first up-close look at the wages of unrealistic debt, I repossessed items that clients had bought with money unwisely borrowed from their grim futures. Sometimes, worst of all, I confiscated goods that clients had once owned free and clear, but which they pledged as collateral on unrealistic loans they now could not pay off.

This, my friends, is experience I undoubtedly would not have accumulated had my career path begun at Harvard Business School.

But I learned so very, very much.

It was not pretty. If I had not desperately needed a job, I doubt that I would have lasted long. My own personal financial situation was enough motive to keep me going. Virtually every day on the streets of Detroit I encountered situations where I could, and often did, say: "There but for the grace of God..." Tragedy is classically defined as the downfall of a great man. But I was working among the people at the bottom of the pile, and there was still room to fall, still tragedy galore. Somehow I had it in my young head that down at the bottom of society there would be some kind of stoic acceptance when it came time to pay the piper, some kind of immunity to embarrassment or humiliation in financial distress. No way. You cannot really understand the agony on the face of a man who is about to lose his manufacturing company unless you have seen the agony on the face of a woman who is about to lose her kitchen table. Or the puzzled eyes of her watching children.

So it was a grim transition from the lakes to the streets of Detroit, working "inside the Boulevard" as the geographical description of the core city was put. In my days as a loan officer, it was a daytime job in the office on Woodward Avenue. The strain was measured there by having to be gatekeeper for our clients' pitiful little excursions into the future. When I moved to repo, however, I became a nighttime prowler, reporting to work at 5 p.m. and cruising the streets to confiscate their purchases. During my time as a collection man and repo man, of course, I had to put on a face, construct my own immunity as much as I could, distance myself as far as possible from the misery at hand. It wasn't a matter of what was right, it was a matter of my own survival. I'm sure cops and ambulance attendants do the same.

Life does go on. And some repo incidents contained a certain bizarre element of humor, and others reflected a certain, well, *swashbuckling* quality.

In one case, I drew the collection card of a woman who was 4 1/2 months behind on payment of a furniture loan. No one had been able to find her at home. Her mother would stand at the door—with the furniture clearly visible behind her—and swear that the daughter did not live at that address. One day, however, I saw the target enter the house. Contact!

Just three knocks on the screen door and I had contact, all right. With not a word spoken, she came flying outside brandishing the largest broom I have ever seen. I fell down, sprawled on the porch, got up and fled to my car—all the while being thrashed on one body part or another by this humongous broom. She used it to beat on the car as I drove away.

I paid a buddy $25 to take over her collection card. About a week later, he showed up bruised. Within a month, that card changed hands perhaps six times.

The nature of my work in the last 20 years has often required me to make announcements which revealed the best possible solution to a major financial problem, but which made scores of people steaming mad. Never again, however, have I been beaten with a broom.

Cars, of course, are the staple of the repo man, the cinematic image of what repo-ing is about. (I can't tell you, by the way, what the symbolism or science fiction of 1984's *Repo Man,* is all about; but I can assure you that Harry Dean Stanton's portrayal of a repo man at work is first-class.)

Back in the '50s, before consumer protection laws introduced certain civilities to the process, the way we did it was nothing short of legalized theft. The company I worked for had a fleet of '57 Fords—300s, or Victorias if you were lucky—with Van Aucken bumpers. We kept a 1 1/2- or two-inch-thick rubber mat in the trunk. When my partner and I found a car to repo, we'd clip the rubber mat onto the Van Aucken, one of us would drive the Ford's right front bumper up to the target car's left rear bumper, the other would smash a vent window on the target car with a ballpeen hammer, hop in and jam the steering wheel to the left. Then we were gone, pushing the repo'ed car into the next neighborhood.

A really good repo crew could accomplish this without hardly bringing the repo car to a halt.

All of our repo cars had radios, and we always made two calls. First, to the towing company to have it come and get the repossessed vehicle. Second, to the police to let them know that the car with the broken vent window was repo'ed, not stolen. Then we'd move on to look for the vehicle on our next repo card.

At least once, I happened to do good by doing well.

Standard procedure was to take personal belongings from a repo'ed car and turn them in the next day. So there was a black suitcase sitting outside in my repo car's trunk when our phone rang about 9 a.m. Joan and I had taken an apartment near City Airport, and I had retreated there to sleep only a few hours earlier after a busy night of repo-ing. My partner and I had capped our shift by grabbing a car that had been on our list for 4 1/2 months. The target car was now sitting in the company garage on Canfield Street, the delinquent party was also there, and my boss was on the phone.

He said the man was demanding his car, had cash to make the payments good, and needed his personal belongings, the black suitcase in particular. In fact, said my boss, the man seemed more interested in his luggage than in his car. I may have been just a young ex-coal handler from Marine City, but this piqued my interest more than a bit.

I dressed, went down to my repo car, got out the suitcase and looked inside. Two handguns. And a whole lot of packets that looked like sugar. Even in the '50s we were sharp enough to know that your average fellow didn't carry coffee sweetener by the suitcase, along with firepower to protect it.

I put the suitcase back in the trunk, went upstairs and called my boss. Don't worry, he said, I'll take care of everything. Just get the suitcase to the garage.

When I pulled up on Canfield, the man was across the street. He came over to me as I opened the trunk and I handed him his prized possession. As he returned to his car—by this time undoubtedly *most* regretful of not making his monthly payments—an army of police officers surrounded him, cuffed him, and led him away.

I later discovered my man was a major pusher. I also realized that if he had known where I lived, he wouldn't have tried to redeem his loot by going through channels.My biggest score as a repo man, however, involved no unusual danger and no exotic cargo. It was a purely intellectual exercise, somewhat like being assigned a Rubik's cube instead of a repo card.

The quarry was a baby blue Cadillac. We knew that Charlie had the car, because other repo crews had seen him driving it. That is a near-useless kind of sighting, however. Unless you want to put your life on the line, what you want is an empty car. Somehow this baby blue Cadillac seemed only to exist when Charlie was behind the wheel.

By the time my partner and I drew the card, there was a $100 bonus out on the Caddy—truly big money in the '50s. The Caddy was perhaps two years old, but it was in top shape and loaded with chrome and gadgets. Charlie had borrowed most of the money he paid for it and, as they say, the loan had "never left the post." Charlie had not made a single payment. Find the Caddy, and my partner and I would have an extra 50 bucks apiece.

It was 1 a.m. and bitter cold. We had been sitting four hours near Charlie's house when I saw a figure in the rear-view mirror. It was Charlie. *Walking.*

Same old pattern. You see Charlie. You see Charlie and the car. You never see just the car. Charlie was whistling his way up his porch. My teeth were chattering too much to whistle. Charlie hadn't been walking very long.

The next morning we followed him. Charlie walked about six blocks and caught a bus. We were baffled.

I was on the afternoon shift about a week later when I decided to drive by the place where Charlie worked. At quitting time, Charlie emerged and . . . caught a bus. More bafflement.

There was more than a $50 bonus at stake here. I was totally intrigued. The lightbulb that finally lit up my brain a few days later was shaped like the destination sign on a city bus. Point A was Charlie's house. Point B was the shop where he worked. The bus that he was hopping would have required a dozen transfers to get from Point A to Point B.

That night I was too excited to sleep. The next morning I was waiting when Charlie came out of the house. I tailed him to the bus stop, and then I tailed the bus. It was a short ride, about 25 blocks. Charlie got out, walked down the street, up a driveway. Then, out of the drive rolled the elusive baby blue Caddy that everyone in the company had been seeking for 90 days!

Charlie drove it to a White Castle about 20 blocks from his workplace, and caught another bus to start his shift—not knowing that this time he would have to ride a bus all the way home. My only regret is that I wasn't there to see the look on his face when he returned to the White Castle.

Such were the colorful episodes in my ground-floor introduction to the world of other people's debt. Most days were not nearly so interesting. Hardly any were so uplifting.

Did I gain experience of the sort that one puts on a resume? Well, yes. I learned the basics of "man's confidence in man," as Dun & Bradstreet once defined credit. I learned the parameters under which one particular company would lend money, how to measure lenders against those parameters, and how to shuffle the paper that got the check written. I learned first-hand what happens when the money does not come back the other way.

Did I gain experience of the sort that one would just as soon not put on a resume? Well, yes. I have never fully come to grips with my youthful repo days. The collateral belonged, in fact, to the finance company. It was right that the lender should get his goods. But there was something seriously wrong with the whole process. Basically, of course, what was wrong is that the money should not have been borrowed in the first place. In many cases it should not have been loaned. Serious lenders accept collateral only to guarantee a loan. They don't *want* your car, your house, your washer and dryer. The finance company would gladly lend $200 against a $2,000 automobile owned free and clear, anticipating repossession of the car when a payment was late. It was legal, but in my book it was criminal.

Did I gain experience of the sort that is so invaluable that one could never summon the words to express it adequately on a resume? Absolutely.

I learned that the temptation to reach into the future is so strong that it causes good people do foolish things.

I learned that the desire to possess whatever baubles your neighbor may possess is so strong that it causes good people to do foolish things.

I learned that debt, once assumed, never goes away.

In all the years since, working with debt at ever higher and more sophisticated levels, I have never found anything to contradict or transcend those basic truths.

Logic would suggest that the two years I spent at the finance company would eventually slide off any synopsis of what I've done and what I do, that my apprenticeship in the pits would somehow become irrelevant. But there are patterns to unrealistic debt, patterns to its effect, patterns to its emotional toll. The end stage of being buried in debt reveals itself in the same ways for day laborers and for top executives, for corner-store partnerships and for multimillion-dollar publicly traded corporations.

Take, as an example, an affluent citizen living life to the full extent of his debt service in a fine suburban home with a jumbo mortgage. His family has more cars, all of them expensive, than his three-car garage will hold. He and his wife belong to the finest clubs and send their children to the finest schools. Every top-shelf electronic gadget known to man is present somewhere in his house, or in his car, or in his vacation retreat. Such a person, very often, defines his very existence by gadgets and baubles. If he encounters a financial crisis that costs him these trappings, he may feel that his very *life* has ended. He is taking a fall from a lofty place, and there is temptation to say that *this* is tragedy, *this* is something different.

I have seen that scenario played out in real life many times, and I will see it many times more. It truly is tragic. But the perspective gained from my basement entrance to the world of finance will never allow me to mark the lofty players of Living in the Future as being somehow unique.

One day I was on a repo crew removing furniture from a house. I was 20 years old. The embarrassment and the weeping and the agony had become familiar. Brutal, but familiar. It was just another repo case until the grandmother collapsed and died of a heart attack as we carted a table out the door.

Barely two years out of high school, I was not yet into formulating theories with names like Living in the Future. But seeds were being sown. I was doing basic research of the most painful type.

Meantime, I continued to struggle with my own personal finances. In a not unusual situation, I was bill collecting while worrying mightily about my own bills.

I also had become a father. It was a difficult pregnancy for Joan, and there was no insurance to pay the medical expenses. Furthermore, life in the city, with a husband who disappeared all night to grab cars from unfortunate debtors, was not quite what she had envisioned married life to be. We decided to retreat back to Port Huron, her hometown, and pursue something more closely resembling a normal life.

Once again I was on the street without a job, and once again the market was bleak.

4

Branching Out

I found a job sailing the lakes because I knew someone on the boats, an uncle. When I needed to make a living ashore, I was hired at the finance company because a friend worked there. When I needed a job back in Joan's hometown, I struck $50-a-week paydirt with a priest.

Father John R. Hogan knew more people than I would meet in five lifetimes. I suspect that, in one way or another, he had helped nearly all of them. I also suspect that he had helped the president of a certain Port Huron bank, or someone dear to the banker. No job openings were readily discernible in 1959, at least not to my naked eye. But after a phone call from Father Hogan to the banker, my finance company experience was deemed just the ticket for entry into a post that had not existed moments before.

We are not talking three-piece suits and large cigars here. My starting weekly salary was exactly equal to the bonus I earned for deducing that Baby Blue Cadillac Charlie's bus was not an express. I was truly grateful for the job, nonetheless. And 33 years later I am even more grateful because, once again, I might just as easily have wound up tuning carburetors in Joe's Garage. The bank position would make two consecutive jobs dealing with credit, advancing to a considerably more respectable forum. A career was being born, whether I knew it or not.

Credit departments in the '50s—even the very end of the '50s—were not exactly the high-profile place to be. The world of commerce had discovered credit, but this newfoundland was more a colony than a superpower. Plastic was not rare but unusual, something for executives to charge meals with, and it carried names like Diner's Club. In most businesses, the credit manager was a nobody—since receivables had not yet become the overwhelming dominant asset on balance sheets.

The consumer population was still awash with customers who paid with currency, or who charged only a small percentage of the purchase. Readers who are old enough will remember the prevalence of "layaway" buying, the now-quaint practice of giving a retailer partial payment to hold an item until the customer could afford it.

Thus, when I started out making consumer loans at the bank, some of the work was of a no-brain variety. Banks are often remembered as being more conservative in those days. That's true. But perhaps more important is that *customers* were more conservative. Most of the consumer loans that I recall going sour involved parents or relatives or friends co-signing loans for young people just starting out in life. It seems the drive to ensure that each succeeding generation would appear more "successful" was making itself visible in the consumer loan department.

The bank was not about to overlook my big-city skills, of course, and I was given the occasional repo job. None of them involved anything as colorful as suitcases of heroin. I did, however, venture all the way to the Upper Peninsula—almost as far away as New York—to sniff out a Cadillac buried in snow at a remote farmhouse. Sunken treasure with body by Fisher.

It's when the bank moved me into commercial loans and real estate development loans that my horizons began to expand. This, too, was a somewhat more sleepy arena than it was to become in succeeding decades. My superiors played many a game of golf with customers, asking "what we can do for you today?" But even in a small-town bank 30 years ago I was able to get meaningful exposure to the intricate, dynamic world of commercial IOUs.

I made and monitored "floor plan" loans to auto dealers. A floor plan is a line of credit through which dealers sell cars they do not own. Floor plans remain today the basis of automobile retailing. The average customer jokes that his new vehicle "belongs to the bank," not realizing that it has belonged to a bank ever since it arrived in the showroom.

The manufacturer sells the car to the dealer, who immediately sends the invoice to the bank. The bank pays the invoice—and owns the car. The dealer pays interest each month while the car sits on his lot, which is why dealers are exceedingly interested in turning over their inventory. When the customer buys the car, the title passes to the dealer momentarily. The buyer then drives out the door under yet another credit arrangement.

The first commercial bankruptcies I saw were car dealers who could not maintain their floor plans. And, in a twist of events I would not have imagined at the finance company, I made my first repo from a dealer. This time, it was an entire floor plan. Bigger stakes, but the principle was the same.

Unserviceable debt in a small community, I discovered, carries its own special agonies. In the city, one must achieve fairly spectacular notoriety before your neighbors are the least aware of who you are. In a small town, the embarrassment of a financial crisis is broadcast on a network based not on Marconi's discovery but on the simple fact that everyone knows everyone. In New York, one would nearly have to be a Donald Trump for one's financial problems to be known by as many people as the difficulties of, say, a mail carrier in a small town.

Somewhere in this milieu, as a "banker" barely into my 20s, I began to realize I had a strong tendency to approach my work holistically. That sounds like so much mumbo-jumbo, but "holistic" is precisely the proper word. In filling out a loan application, I didn't see just a name and a set of criteria to be met before cutting a check. I saw an entire situation—an applicant and his set of problems and needs, and my employer, the bank, with its goals and standards to be met. As early as the finance company days I had tried to help clients from a third-party point of view. I asked applicants if they were sure they wanted to extend themselves to buy an appliance or a used car that they might be able to do without. At the bank, unaware at first that I was charting a course for a life's work, I began to take it further.

My consumer clients at the bank generally had more assets, and thus more flexibility. I would analyze an applicant's options, show them other alternatives. I would ask them to define their goals, to be sure they knew why they were asking for a loan. In a few cases, I talked them out of borrowing money.

Working with auto dealers and other relatively small firms in the commercial department I gained my first exposure to *companies* in trouble. It was to the bank's benefit to make sure the clients got *out* of trouble. So I went into the trenches with them as they juggled balls of debt and struggled to find ways to keep the balls airborne. Almost from the beginning, the key to the trick seemed to be: *Don't toss yet another ball into the air.*

It seemed too simple. But in the years ahead, with the opportunity to view financial crises from every possible angle, and in much greater magnitude, I would find it to be absolutely correct. When the juggler has put in motion a construction so shaky that he is staggering in circles beneath it, it is usually not the best idea to toss up another ball just to see what will happen.

"Bill consolidation loans" were very popular in the '50s and '60s. The terminology remains current, but it seemed more prevalent in those days, as more and more people got caught up in the credit machine for the first time. Here was a case where I gladly counseled customers to take out a loan, because—used properly—bill consolidation schemes make much good sense.

If you are $10,000 in debt and your monthly payments are $1,000, but you can afford to pay only $500, then you have to consolidate your obligations and make the lower payment. But obviously it will take you twice as long to pay. And during that time the last thing you should do is toss another ball into the air. Far too often, that is exactly what happens. The trouble occurs in the first place because the debtor is living too far into the future. He consolidates his debt and—aha!—sees an opportunity to extend even further into the future. His plastic is no longer on hold, for example, so he foolishly runs out and uses it.

In financial terminology, debt consolidation loans often generate "excess positive cash flow," which is then abused. In the '50s, common terminology was more basic. If someone did not pay, he was a "deadbeat." Today a deadbeat is said to have "cash-flow problems." And he usually goes shopping for more "leverage."

Living on a low-level bank salary, I had my own cash-flow problems and no difficulty empathizing with my loan customers. With medical bills accumulating and a second child on the way, it wasn't a matter of putting myself in the shoes of someone having a financial crisis. I was wearing the same brand of brogans. My own finances would be shaky for the first decade of our marriage.

I have always paid my bills and have never cashed an unemployment check, two facts I in which I maintain some pride. Lest you discount that as typical reminiscence from a man living comfortably in middle age, you should know that it was a close call. I came very close to personal bankruptcy on more than one occasion, and there was pain and agony in avoiding it. There always is. When you finally decide not to throw one more ball into the air, there is pain and agony. Sometimes the result *is* formal bankruptcy. If you make the decision soon enough, tighten the belt and live within your means, reorganization will likely solve the problem. Either way, there is much pain and much agony. Accompanied, fortunately, by much relief and much self-esteem.

One of the very first financial situations that I reorganized was my own. Most painfully, it involved giving up the house we had bought and using what precious little equity we had accrued to help pay bills. We moved to a smaller, very old place—and barely could afford to keep it heated.

It seemed clear that drawing one paycheck, at least *my*

paycheck, was not the best of all possible ways to keep moving that monthly pile of envelopes off the shelf.

I attacked the situation with the vigor of a field marshal engaged on many fronts. I sought more paychecks, and I sought better paychecks. At one point I had five income sources, ranging from lawnmowing to the position that appears on my resume. For a decade, I walked overlapping paths as I worked toward putting my own financial life in an ever more solvent position.

The first path was logical and traditional. I made a series of career moves to better jobs. By both design and fortuitousness, each new job revealed a new corner of the credit machine to explore:

- Retail credit, at Sears—which in 1962 still included Roebuck in its logo. I dealt with all the structures that allow retailers to move goods without cash changing hands, working with customers and their problems, working with the financial side of the company and *its* cash-flow concerns. Even here I was involved in some repossessing. Unserviced debt, it seems, produces basically the same result whether it involves pushing a Van Aucken bumper against a used Buick in the dead of night or liquidating the assets of a Fortune 500 company.

- Industrial credit, at Peninsular Steel—a well-respected Detroit company in whose service I was always proud to lay my card on a client's desk. This was business-to-business credit, of the kind that lubricates that great engine called the manufacturing economy. Here I first participated, in all its intricacies, in the debt world that lies beyond the "first secured creditor"—translate, "bank." When you supervise a customer's credit in this arena, and your customer becomes financially troubled, your company must take a number and wait in line to see if the receivable will materialize.

- Diversified industrial credit, at Automatic Sprinkler Corp. of America—a Cleveland firm where, as assistant to the corporate director of credit, I traveled extensively dealing with 32 affiliated companies throughout the U.S. I handled accounts receivable and liquidations, and supervised the most serious receivables at many of the various subsidiaries. On my own, I began to develop properties for syndication.

- Paragon Steel, back in Detroit, where I drew my last payroll check and where I served initially as credit manager, assistant treasurer and president of a subsidiary, Paragon Resources. The company placed tremendous emphasis on its most important asset, accounts receivable. I was directly responsible for—and involved almost daily in—a number of debt restructurings. This was vital to the survival not only of Paragon's customers, but of Paragon itself.

Each of those positions had its rewards in experience and, as time progressed, salary. You could say that they add up to my employment resume. Over the same period, however, I was busy compiling a unique *self-employment* resume.

This was the second path, an evolutionary career whose genesis cannot be pinpointed—though it probably dates to the first time I told a finance company loan applicant that "maybe you can find a better way."

In less prehistoric and less vague terms, perhaps it began with the Port Huron automobile dealer for whom I developed a restructuring plan. To my recollection, that is the first time I offered advice to someone in financial trouble, for a fee, billed in my name.

At one time in the early days I may have been the only card-carrying financial consultant in the country who was also earning a full-time paycheck and, by the way, tending a lawn (that of industrialist Dick Morand) across the road. As I said, it was an *evolutionary* process.

The synergy of my two career paths was total. Each new task I assumed for an employer complemented the abilities I could bring to a client as a consultant. Every case I took on as a consultant meant experience beyond the narrower boundaries of whatever shop I was working in.

Criss-cross all the stops on both paths of my detailed resume and you would find a remarkable number of definable job descriptions, tasks and contexts. But all involve two things: Debt and trouble. Like ham and eggs.

You would also find some interesting and substantial footnotes—such as syndicating more than 50 co-partnerships. In recent years I have taken to saying, "I used to syndicate partnerships as a hobby." I guess what I mean is it was something that did not involve coping with troubled debt—which is where I began, where I delved into ever higher and more complex manifestations of the phenomenon, and where I now devote perhaps 95 percent of my time.

As my consulting work evolved, there was no name for it. My business all came by word of mouth. The word wasn't "turnaround specialist," or "distressed debtor consultant." It would be more like:

"Why don't you talk to Jim McTevia? I think he can help you."

"Oh? What is he?"

"He's a numbers man."

"What's his title?"

"Doesn't have one."

"What's his education?"

"Doesn't have one."

"Why would I want to have him help me?"

"Well, because he's helped a lot of people."

It takes time, experience and a fair amount of success to build a business that way.

By the time I had been at Peninsular Steel a couple of years, my consulting business had begun to look like a potentially serious endeavor. Peninsular gave me my first opportunities to represent an unsecured creditor, Peninsular, at those ominous creditors' meetings where the fate of the debt-ridden customer rides in the balance—the forum where the public typically first gets an inkling that a once-solid corporate citizen is swinging in the wind. It was Peninsular that gave me my first opportunity to work closely with troubled major customers, helping them find ways to stay afloat—at the same time, of course, protecting the credit Peninsular had granted the customer. And if the customer liked what he saw, he was a potential client for my consulting work beyond Peninsular's interests.

One such client wrote to the president of Peninsular in April 1966:

> "Had it not been for the vision and tireless work of Jim McTevia, we might have been out of business two weeks ago. Jim entered the picture just as a combination of circumstances (such as an uncontrollable accounts payable position, a lack of working capital, and our local bank's refusal to discount any additional receivables) had backed us to the wall.
>
> "He studied our books, our sizeable order backlog and our productive facilities...and engineered and set up a plan working night and day that would enable me to salvage the company into which I have poured 20 years of my life, the company founded by my grandfather in 1893."

I spend a major part of my workday reading and reciting cold numbers and telling people cold facts they don't want to hear. So it probably often stretches credibility when I tell clients that it is the *human* element of their troubles—of the whole numbers game called Living in the Future—that is so important to me. But my heirs will find this moldy letter in my desk drawer. Whatever money I made from the case was spent 26 years ago.

Peninsular, of course, was happy to receive the letter. I —as the Peninsular employee who had approved at least part of the credit at risk—was ecstatic. The troubled customer was operating as a solid company a quarter century later.

It was in my early days at Peninsular, by the way, that I was working five jobs. The lawnmowing paid for gas to make the 130-mile daily round-trip jaunt between Port Huron and Detroit.

5

A Profession Is Born

If you own a business, you can check the screen of your desktop PC and find out exactly how much revenue is past due from which customers. Your credit manager should be able to answer your next question: *Why* isn't the customer paying his bill?

Working in credit and answering the "Why?" question is one good explanation of how I came to do what I do.

Ask your delinquent customers why their accounts are past 90 days and you will seem to get more responses than there are 18-wheelers on the nearest freeway. But—assuming the money is truly owed, and the customer has no quarrel with the goods or services rendered—the responses all come down to two situations.

"I can't pay."

Or "I won't pay."

Forget about "won't." That's a no-brainer. He's a deadbeat, and his account goes to the collection department for the usual dreary process.

"Can't" is an entirely different story. These are people who *want* to pay, who are distressed as a result of Living in the Future, and whose situations require investigation and analysis. How far they have dipped into the future will determine whether it is too late to stop the loss of blood—whether you can ever get paid, and whether they can stay in business.

This tidy little analysis, by the way, works exactly the same for individuals as it does for companies.

Companies, or people, live as far into the future as their debt service will allow. At some point, the Ponzi scheme reveals itself in the form of trouble with creditors. The problem can be addressed—or it can be allowed to straggle on to its inevitable conclusion, which is bankruptcy.

In the '60s, and before, that basically meant Bankruptcy Court under the old Bankruptcy Act. And that meant a black hole from which, once sucked in, very few emerged. Bankruptcy was socially unacceptable, economically inviable, something to be avoided at all costs.

This was obviously not a bad time for a young man to be developing a reputation for helping companies to pull back from the vortex. To say I was creating a profession in the process is just another way of saying nobody else was doing what I was doing. That is amazing—because if necessity is the mother of invention, then Thomas Edison would have died of circuit over-load as a credit manager in the '60s. Answering the "why?" question brought me, every day, into the offices of businessmen who needed a turnaround specialist, a distressed debtor consult-ant, or whatever terminology you might apply to this then non-existent profession.

The stench of bankruptcy in those days, however, was so strong that it kept practitioners of all stripes away from even the periphery of troubled situations. No one wanted to deal openly with people having financial problems. Not one major accounting firm wanted to deal with a company in serious financial distress. Today, every one of the Big Eight has a specialty department to work with troubled companies, and all are listed in the directory of the Turnaround Management Association. They don't do what I do, but that's another story for Part Two.

Throughout the '60s and into the '70s I was very much alone in the field, wearing various hats as employee and consultant and entrepreneur and bankruptcy receiver, asking the "why?" question, sorting companies with problems that could be addressed from those that had strayed too far into the future to be helped.

By 1970, if someone in the next seat on the red-eye asked what I did for a living I might say something like: "I'm a credit executive, I do consulting, and I have my own companies."

That entrepreneurial facet of my resume has become an inactive one, even though today—at a time when I have some money and some substantial lines of credit available—I constantly see worthwhile companies that I could pick up for almost nothing. These are firms that will be back on their feet and thriving if they get some help working out a plan with creditors and some time to reorganize, and if they display a willingness to take the tough financial steps necessary to live within their means. I help them do just that, but I resist any temptation to step into an ownership role.

That has not always been the case.

My very first manufacturing company acquisition shaped up as a full-bore disaster until, after a series of nightmarish surprises and sleepless nights, I escaped with a wash.

It was a small family-owned business in central Michigan. Financial data revealed that the company had posted consistent profits over the years, despite substantial wages and benefits drawn by the principals. They were three brothers—two in their late 70s and one, the chief operating officer and the wisest of the clan, in his mid-80s. The trio had operated the place for three decades.

My plan was to buy the shop and get rich.

The brothers were interested in selling because of their age. And they were willing to sell to someone who would put just a little cash down and repay them the balance over time. Yes, the chronicler of Living in the Future was about to dive—to belly-flop—into a leveraged buyout.

The brothers wanted to take all of the existing cash out of the company, so—besides the minimal down payment—I would need some working capital. Because this was my first acquisition, because I was young and didn't know any better, it seemed so simple. I borrowed the money. The way it looked to me, all I had to do was continue operations at the status quo and watch the money flow in to pay for my new industrial outpost.

The owners agreed to stay on and help my new manager through a break-in period. The chief operating officer, who knew everything about the financial side of the company, agreed to help for a full year. I should have suspected that the old gentleman would not be able "to live up to his part of the bargain" when, at the closing, he continually had to lie down while signing papers. When he died soon thereafter, I had lost a key source of guidance.

There I sat, the highly leveraged owner of a company I knew very little about—and which no living man knew very well. Because this was a venture capital acquisition, and because I was involved with other businesses as well as consulting, I could not spend much time on-site. On the other hand, I was a specialist in troubled companies, and this wasn't a troubled company. It had a decent work force and a pretty good backlog of orders. I had hired my own manager. Everything still seemed okay.

Within 12 months I had found several skeletons in every closet. By today's standards, the shop was an environmental disaster. The machinery and equipment were in sad need of repair or, in some cases, replacement. It was a union shop, but the former owners had always been in a financial position to shut the place down and go out of business if the employees pushed too hard. That was certainly not an alternative for me, because all profits for the foreseeable future were earmarked to pay my debt to the former owners.

The employees, who saw that I was a young man, figured I must be awfully well-heeled to have bought the place where they worked. So they expected that a strike threat would generate substantial wage increases.

More importantly, I learned that a great deal of the company's profits over the years had been produced by the former owners coming in after hours and on weekends to generate the extra volume that made the bottom line look so good.

Obviously, I was rapidly becoming a potential client for

my own consultancy. Unfortunately, I did not have the standard consultant's option in case things do not go well: Moving on to the next client. In this case, if I was wrong, my credibility as someone who could keep a financially troubled firm out of bankruptcy was about to be totally destroyed.

After agonizing over every conceivable business problem during that first year, I found yet another problem—and it became clear that my company was, in fact, headed for bankruptcy.

I learned that one of our major customers was angry that he hadn't had an opportunity to buy the company when the three brothers let it go. He made it known in conversation from time to time that he possessed great expertise in running companies. Further, if we couldn't provide him with product at a reduced rate, he would be forced to open his own plant. Trying to deal with this man was like trying to deal with an armed and hungry cannibal on a very small desert island. Eventually you are going to be served up on a platter. I was either going to lose a major customer's business, or I would keep the business but on an unprofitable basis.

This last piece of the nightmarish puzzle was the straw that *spared* the camel's back. That's because, in revealing a very large ego and a great deal of greed, my latest tormentor in this enterprise also inspired my saving strategy.

I developed a plan where my little company was sold to my bullish customer for exactly the amount of my investment. I agreed to finance it for six months. At the end of six months, I was even—and out. At the end of a year, the company went bankrupt.

At a young age I made my narrowest escape from a difficult situation. And I learned a number of important lessons the hard way before making any further investments.

First, I learned that any analysis of a business situation must be something more than cursory. A steady line of profits— or losses—does not in itself signal what lies around the bend. Any risks must be carefully identified.

Second, I never again entered a venture without making

certain that sufficient funds were available to weather almost any conceivable storm.

Third, from that point forward I never became involved in a business venture by myself. I was always willing to share the obvious impending windfall with partners—who would also share in any unforeseen bad times. This became my cardinal business rule. As lucrative as an opportunity might seem, don't get greedy. Share the wealth. Share the pain.

In the '60s and '70s, as I syndicated various business partnerships, I became known in southeastern Michigan as the Kresge of partnership syndications. All of my syndicates had numerous individual partners, each with an investment of a reasonable size. The total of each syndicate, however, represented a very substantial portfolio. None of the syndicates was connected to the others.

In more recent years, I became less and less eager to participate in the entrepreneurial struggles I saw on the street. One major exception occurred in the early '80s, when I found a virtually bankrupt company that was buried in debt amid the 20 percent interest climate of the time. It was losing money. The company's bank wanted out. The people inside the company were very good at doing what the company did, but were about to drown in the financial tide. After careful analysis, it looked to me like a good company to own and to reorganize.

I and a group of my friends formed an investment company and bought the struggling firm for $750,000. I personally went out and dealt one on one with all the major creditors, restructured all the debt, found new financing, and gave the people in the company time to make it work. To make a medium-length story short, we sold it after five years for $16 million. There were many happy shareholders. The people running the company did very well. Smiles all around.

Aside from the personal cash we put into the venture, Joan and I jointly and severally guaranteed a very large sum of money to a new lender for working capital. If the venture failed, we would have paid dearly. It was a risky, fulfilling, lucrative experience. But I have absolutely no regrets for not following that path more often.

For one thing, I want to be known as someone who helps troubled companies, not someone who is sniffing out investment opportunities. Clients struggling to find their last, best hope are not likely to enter waters where they perceive sharks to be on patrol. I have made it a rule never to mix my consulting practice with a business venture, a posture for which I have become well-known. People experiencing serious financial difficulties go through tremendous stress and emotional problems, and are willing to grasp at straws. Somebody is always waiting to take advantage of a company that is financially weak, and an owner who is distraught. That somebody will not be our firm.

For another thing, to dabble seriously as an entrepreneur I would have to go on the line for some debt. I choose not to live in the future, playing a game with no object but to run up my estate's net worth. I strongly believe we are all here to make a certain product or to perform a certain service, to *contribute* something. McTevia rule number two is that, if at all possible, you should be doing something you enjoy. To be productive *and* enjoying yourself is, to my mind, as good as it gets.

What I truly enjoy is channeling my experiences into a service that makes the best of a bad situation, that helps people in the only way I know how. The careful observer might see me entering a creditors' meeting to speak to 50 or so people who, literally, are going to ask for the keys to my client's business for the purpose of shutting it down. Or might eavesdrop on a conversation with two honest people who have worked very hard for a very long time and whom I must tell that it is time to wind down their entrepreneurial creation, to withdraw now with dignity instead of later with even greater heartbreak—and debt. "Good grief, McTevia," the careful observer might rightly ask, "just what is your definition of 'enjoy'?"

Well, this is the big "enjoy," the one that lets you sleep well at night, the one that in your bolder moments lets you describe yourself as "fulfilled." Yes, I make a comfortable living.

But I do sleep well at night. And, at least when I am able to help a client, I feel fulfilled.

At this stage of my life, I indulge myself in the small "enjoy," too. I enjoy the present to the fullest extent possible, without letting that enjoyment interfere with my professional practice. In fact, I undoubtedly plow more of my income right back into the present than any financial adviser would recommend.

Even if it were not an unwise signal to my potential clients, even if I were more willing to live in the future, I do not think I would be eager to dabble in venture capitalism again. I know the failure rate. I don't think I'm a better widget-maker than the next guy. It's the people who know their widgets best who are most likely to be able to put their companies back on course, given a sound financial plan. If business were an easy proposition, there would be no employees. We'd all buy a widget factory, put it on auto pilot, and go out to play.

It is important that I *have* been an entrepreneur, however, because it takes my arc of experience the full 360 degrees. The circle is complete. I can walk into any troubled business situation and honestly tell anyone at the table—banker, creditor, entrepreneur, officer of the court—that I have sat exactly where they are sitting. I have been the person whose loan was at risk. I have been the person whose investment was at risk. I have been the duly appointed representative of the government who is to make certain that no fraud or preference in payment of creditors is present. I have reorganized companies and I have liquidated companies. I have done that in court and I have done that out of court. Any direction you want to take this case, I can tell you what will happen. Now, here's my plan.

It's more complex than that, as you will see in Part Three. But simply put, there is no hat I have not worn in this painful process—from repo man to receiver, from bill collector to credit manager, from anxious creditor to anxious entrepreneur. Very few entrepreneurs, in fact, could have been more anxious than I was in that very first venture—with my machinery crumbling and my employees eager for higher wages and my largest customer threatening to walk and my credit line stretched to the last decimal point. When I tell my troubled clients that I understand the agony they are going through, I am not blowing hot air.

I removed the hat of employee for the final time in 1976. As I became better known, bankruptcy attorneys had begun to recommend me to the courts. There was plenty of work to be done as receiver under the old Bankruptcy Act, and it was not possible to do so while affiliated with a company that could present a conflict of interest along a troubled company's chain of creditors. So I left Paragon Steel, hung up my shingle and became, to the best of my knowledge, the first consultant to go into business full-time seeking clients among companies on the verge of bankruptcy.

First, in the '60s, it was a business card that simply said: "James V. McTevia." Then it became "James V. McTevia & Associates." The underline reads: "Management and Adjustment Consultants." We are *not* in the insurance adjusting business. The adjustment refers to *debt*.

Companies and people—people possessing all the outward trappings of "success"—come to us and tell us:

"I can't pay."

With the creditor wolves howling at the door for what is rightfully theirs, we try to buy a little time. Every minute of that week or 30 days or 90 days is precious, because we use it to answer—dispassionately, from *our* research, not from the client's—the old credit manager's question: "Why?"

We analyze where the company (or person) has been, where it is now, and where it is likely to be in one year. If our analysis shows that it is not too late to tighten the belt, to withdraw from unrealistic Living in the Future, then we work with the client, the banks and the creditors to implement a survival plan. If the damage is too great, if too much blood has been let, we wind it down in the most orderly, equitable manner possible.

That is the perspective you will see in Part Three. In Part Two, you'll see how the same dynamics are at work in your personal financial life. And in Part Four, with your indulgence,

I'd like to raise some serious questions about Living in the Future's horrible impact on generations yet to come.

If I make too many analogies to ambulance drivers or cops or cancer surgeons, I think perhaps by this point you can understand why. You see a lot of distress in my business. It is, in fact, virtually the only thing you see. And when you see a *cause* of distress as frequently as ambulance drivers smell alcohol or cancer surgeons smell cigarette smoke, then it is your duty to try to tell the story. Particularly when there is no surgeon general or MADD out there trumpeting the message.

Mine is not an easy message to swallow. Even my clients don't want to hear it. Often I believe they listen for only two reasons: They've paid me a handsome fee, and they have run out of lines to cast into the future.

Why should I be surprised? After all, it took me half a lifetime of unique experience to comprehend the lesson taught so well by the Blonde Goddess so many years ago.

PART TWO

Individuals in Trouble

6

Putting the 'Personal' in Finances

Debt transcends income, gender, ethnicity, religious belief, political affiliation or Zip Code. Every American has a lifelong relationship with debt.

Most of us cannot live without some form of personal debt, no matter our resolve or our financial means to try.

Used properly, debt can be a valuable tool. It can make certain of our daily affairs more practical. It can achieve a better outcome on our IRS 1040. It can allow us to go out on a reasonable and strong limb to secure something very important to us. It can make the complex thing we call "running a business" possible.

Used improperly, debt can resolve any question you might have about the existence of hell by putting you there long before your time. Unrealistic debt can be an emotional burden you never talk about, even while it affects every minute of your life.

In any case, our elected officials in Washington have made debt a cradle-to-grave proposition. Every infant in every hospital nursery owes, at this writing, a $17,000 share of federal debt. That's an average year's take-home pay—more than two years' worth at minimum wage.

Considering the constant new borrowing, much of it from foreign lenders, to pay the *interest* on this debt; considering the reluctance of Washington to reverse its credit binge of recent decades; and considering that, therefore, my share and your share of this debt appear likely to grow before being dumped on the next generation—today's babies have plenty of reason to cry. When they are old enough to talk and express an opinion on the subject, they will shout back at us through the pages of history: "Why did you mortgage me?"

If today's infants behave like other recent generations, however, their own private accounts will be run up at an awesome pace. At the end of the life cycle, they will realize that many of our personal debts also outlive us. You may become unburied from debt in the time-honored tradition: by being buried in the ground. Your heirs, however, will have to deal with your obligations. Even a Rockefeller operating on a pure cash basis will leave a month's utility bills for the estate to settle.

Between cradle and grave, personal debt and how we handle it is our lowest common denominator. Technology has produced all kinds of Big Brother capabilities for monitoring our lives, but the only one anybody seems to care much about—the one by far most prized or reviled—is our credit rating. Only our spouses know more about us than a pair of alphabet institutions that monitor the nation's indebtedness. One (TRW) keeps track of debt we asked for. Another (IRS) keeps track of debt we didn't ask for.

This lifelong relationship with debt is hardly as important as our relationships with people. *Unrealistic* debt, however, seriously affects personal relationships. Ask, for example, any marriage counselor. Money problems, meaning unrealistic debt, shatter marriages. Sexual problems? Perhaps it's a tie; who really knows? But be sure to ask the counselor how many sexual problems—or "communication" problems—are caused by money problems.

We call it *"personal* finance," but somehow regard it as impersonal. We entrust our souls to the clergy, and our psyches to the psychologists, but our personal finances we turn over to a "numbers man." A good numbers man sees beyond this fallacy. The fact is, mere numbers on a few pieces of paper invade every aspect of our lives, directly or indirectly. Our personal finances influence how we feel about ourselves, whether we sleep well or not, whether an underlying anxiety persists on the sunniest of days.

The book racks and talk shows are filled with personal advice on self-esteem and on money matters. Usually the two topics are treated as being no more intertwined than geography and needlepoint. That is a serious mistake. The vast majority of these money books and money lecturers focus solely on *How to (Fill in the Blank) and Get Rich.* That is an even more serious mistake.

It is not the size of our income that most radically affects our emotional lives; it is how far we are financially Living in the Future. The sad truth is that a large percentage of Americans would feel truly reborn if they could just start over, no longer up to their nose in debt. That is true whether their annual salary is $20,000, $50,000 or $150,000. Buried is buried. If you are suffocating, you don't much care how deep you are buried. You just want to breathe.

Probably just one demographic group will have absolutely no use for this discussion. The truly poor, a significant but thankfully still small minority, have very little opportunity to live in the future. The problems of those in poverty are monstrous, but overreaching at the credit window is not a central issue.

Logic suggests that the truly wealthy, those who need hired help to determine how many assets they control, should also be excluded. Surely someone whose today is extremely large won't encourage trouble by dipping too far into his or her tomorrow. Tomorrow is, after all, an unknown entity for *all* of us. Alas, even people of genuine wealth sometimes pay the price of Living in the Future, as you will see shortly.

Two important concepts must be kept in mind, then, as we take a serious look at personal finances: how they become troubled, and how to dig out from trouble.

First, we are discussing a *personal* subject. It is not something to be contemplated merely in terms of numbers, nor something that can be relegated to your accountant or to one hair-raising night a month with your checkbook and a stack of bills. We are talking about personal well-being in a sense far more important than the number of suits in your closet. And we are talking about basic personal behavior that cannot be maintained as easily as seeing that your vehicle gets put through the car wash from time to time.

Second, it is a subject that demands attention from all of us. It is not a matter of factory wages versus upper middle-class salaries. We would all prefer to be on the receiving end of the larger number, of course. But that is not what Living in the Future is about. It's a self-inflicted disease that is contracted just as often, if not more often, by citizens whose incomes far exceed the median. Those who are "better off" actually suffer the disease's most virulent strain.

The problem, and therefore the solution, is so simple as to approach absurdity. I tell that to my clients—most of whom these days are principals of companies in trouble, but whose companies' problems closely resemble those of individuals in trouble.

Over the years I have developed highly specialized, talented associates and staff members. We have computers. We utilize the best accounting and legal support. We analyze every case with acumen derived from decades of experience. We punch out spreadsheets by the pound. We produce sophisticated, custom-tailored reports and business plans that accurately portray the best path for damage control, and the likely outcome. As the end product of our labors, these are among the highest-priced volumes in the land. For the cost of one such report, you could purchase an entire press run of this book. Nonetheless, the advice in every report to every one of my clients boils down to three options:

First, you can reduce expenses.

Second, you can increase income.

Third, you can do both.

That's it. Period. There is no other way to deal with a troubled financial situation. Those three options represent thousands of dollars worth of advice for a troubled company, so they certainly ought to be worth a dime or two for a troubled individual.

The most slender of equations, of course, often requires the greatest effort from the beholder. One need not be a CPA, an attorney or an economist to figure out those three options. A fifth-grader could probably produce the theory. It is that obvious. Nonetheless, people devise ever more sophisticated means to defy a simple truth that is as sound as Newton's Law. You would be amazed—and will be, I hope, before we are finished—to understand why someone of my background cannot help but view our society as an implausibly gravity-defying enterprise.

No one, of course, sets out purposely to find financial trouble. So we'll have to keep digging here for more insight.But keep those three simple options in mind. They are golden. And there are no substitutes.

7

First, You Jog

If you have never slipped into a pair of Nikes and jogged, not even down to the corner and back, no one need warn you against competing in a marathon tomorrow. The best result would be acute embarrassment. At worst, you would kill yourself.

That's the bad news.

The good news is that you probably *can* run a marathon. You just need to get yourself in position for the effort. You must build up endurance, all the while measuring your ability to step up to the next and longer distance.

Basically, that is all there is to financial fitness. Think of the marathon as being whatever creature comforts, toys and housing accommodations you regard as necessary for "the good life." You can build up your strength and get there, over time. Or you can go chasing after all the trophies immediately. It might not kill you; then again, it might. Either way, it *will* put your financial life into cardiac arrest.

At some point—either after high school or after college—we go into serious training for this financial marathon. Before then, we barely jog. But when the schooling is over and the independent living begins, we're running down that road for real. We have competitors. Many of us hit the road jealous of those who have the trophies that go with completing the full distance.

In this financial marathon only one measure of endurance

matters, and that is income. It is truly incredible how many people with a two-mile bank account will sprint out for an assault on the full 26 miles. They "hit the wall" and wind up on a stretcher before the rest of the field even gets into stride. With luck, they will run again; but only if they start training again from scratch, jogging a block or two at a time.

I've used the marathon analogy many times in speeches. That's inevitable. Runners have a lot of time to think, I'm a runner, and I make my living thinking about finances. The marathon analogy is a simplistic one, but it strikes me as entirely accurate and useful.

I decided to start running—literal, physical running—several years ago. At first I struggled to get around the block. Within a year, after building up my legs and my cardiovascular strength, I was able to run a 10 kilometer race comfortably. In middle age, it was fascinating to see how my own body could be brought that far through proper endurance training. This is not a bragging point. On some weekends, in fact, it seems that half the population has discovered the wonders of 10K racing. The point is, I can't help relating it to personal finances. Sometimes, as I'm cruising down the street and thinking back to how I increased my endurance, I look around at my fellow racers and wonder how many are leading a marathon lifestyle on a 10K income.

The financial marathon more often is called "the rat race," a striking image but not such a useful one. Casualties of the rat race, after all, are those who defy the marathon equation: endurance (income) = distance (solvency). You can overload the left side of the equation and prosper. Overload the right side, however, and your financial life dies. You will be bankrupt, whether or not you have hired an attorney to make it official.

When you leave the shelter of your parents' home, you start incurring financial obligations. Things that once were mere concepts—heat, lights, water, rent, a refrigerator that doesn't fill itself—suddenly are realities. You *haven't bought a thing,* and you are incurring expenses! Probably you have car payments to make. That's six hefty bills without a single pizza ordered!

What it is, my young friend, is time for a serious endurance check. Chances are that the right side of the equation has drawn perilously near to equalling the left. You're probably at best a 4K runner right now. Don't try to run any farther!

If the marathon equation is unbalanced, only three strategies can prevent a financial coronary: increase endurance, or decrease distance, or do both.

It's those three familiar and simple rules, dressed in sweats and running shoes.

As a young adult, my own financial marathon equation became seriously unbalanced. I at least give myself credit for making every effort to bring the equation back into balance. The usual way to boost endurance is to get a raise, or find a better-paying job. Nice work if you can get it. I used every equalizing method known to man. I did get raises and I did get better jobs. I also worked several jobs at once. (My media and marketing consultant, who knows me quite well in my current professional life, was astounded to learn in these pages that years ago I mowed lawns while crunching numbers). I also sold assets. I also *decreased* my lifestyle.

Such were the inclinations of a child of the '50s who got caught Living in the Future.

Times change. A popular book on the market as I write this volume has triggered a flurry of articles suggesting that Americans work too many hours. Perhaps. Certainly there is not much space for "quality time" if all one does is work and sleep. The immutable fact remains that, no matter how one views the concept of "too much work" aesthetically, the marathon equation never changes. The aesthetic of Living in the Future is universally ugly. No quality can be found in time that is mortgaged, no joy in trying to run 26 miles on five miles worth of gas.

Some of us live to work. Some of us work to live. Most of us fall somewhere in between. Any spot on that scale is a valid choice. No one is required to run the full financial marathon. Your inner peace and self-esteem, however, rest squarely on your obligation to complete the distance in which you have chosen to race today. When you sign up to run, you know exactly how far your endurance can take you. You should compete at a somewhat *shorter* distance than your maximum, leaving yourself some energy in reserve.

If a couple or a family finds themselves struggling in a rat race, they must honestly analyze whether they are caught by circumstances beyond their control—meaning physical disability, a tornado or such. More often, they have chosen to run a distance beyond their endurance. A $40,000-a-year family living in a $100,000-a-year home, for instance, will of necessity have to "work too much." Such a family immediately should say, "Hey! What are we doing in the marathon? Let's get realistic and run the 10K."

Perhaps the marathon equals a four-bedroom ranch and two cars, while the 10K equals a bungalow with one car and a bus pass. So be it. The equation measures only capabilities, not aspirations. Capability is the present. Aspiration is the future. Live there at your great peril.

In the real world of road running, by the way, my choice has been not to compete in a marathon. I am just as pleased with my 10K efforts as the marathoners or the *ultra*marathoners are with their more distant achievements. I know what kind of endurance it takes to run 26 miles or more, and I choose not to invest the discipline and effort. I think I *could* run a marathon, but not today.

If I ever choose to go the full distance, I'll get that equation balanced first.

8

Till Debt Do Us Part

Of all the contracts entered into by human beings, marriage is by far the most demanding. It also, and sadly, is one of society's most frequently severed contracts. I am not, thank God, a marriage counselor. Throughout my career, however, I have watched these lifetime contracts collapse as a direct result of financial problems.

My clients today tend to be business principals in serious financial trouble, with companies and upscale lifestyles hanging precariously in the balance. Such dramatic financial scenarios can topple and shatter a marriage, like a vase crashing from a shelf. Those instances are just the tip of the iceberg. More typically, and at all income strata, a bad financial situation slowly grinds up a marriage and leaves the pieces strewn along the way.

Today, with Living in the Future prevalent and traditional aversion to credit a dimming memory, more and more couples are entering the marriage contract with 2.9 strikes against them. A newlywed couple is far more likely to bring two incomes—and two mortgaged futures—to the altar. Chances are good that they will blame each other for the financial moment of truth that lies ahead.

That is not to say, however, that financial problems are an

invention of the '80s, or that finances have not always been a likely cause of a broken marriage. One case from early in my career has stayed in mind for years as an archetypical study in how not to approach life's marathon as a couple.

John and Mary Parsons (not their real names, of course) had been married about three years when I met them. I was a young loan officer and was challenged by their particular circumstances as loan applicants.

John worked in a local factory and had become accustomed to a large amount of overtime pay, which almost doubled his income. Mary was secretary to an officer at a savings and loan association. They had no children and, between the two of them, a rather substantial income by anyone's standards in the early '60s.

However, they also had a new home, for which they had borrowed a down payment from Mary's parents; two cars, both with sizeable mortgages; an FHA home improvement loan, which had been used to pay for landscaping, fencing and a two-car garage; a Sears revolving credit account; a Sears easy payment account; a J.C. Penney charge account, and two gasoline credit cards. All John and Mary "lacked" were national all-purpose credit cards, a phenomenon then in its infancy.

What they sought from my bank, through me, was a bill consolidation loan. They were approximately my age and made four times as much money. What in the world did they do with their income?

As I reviewed their application, I knew John and Mary either had cash tucked away in a mattress or perhaps in Switzerland—or they were guilty of squandering money and living far, far beyond their means. The application, and a frank discussion with them, made it clear that the latter was the case.

Unfortunately for them, and fortunately for me, Mary let slip that the main reason for the bill consolidation was that she was four months pregnant and would be leaving her job within 60 days. They wanted "to get their finances in order before starting to raise a family."

Being a loan officer at one of only two banks in a small

Midwestern community is a most unenviable position. You are dealing with people you know, or whose families you know; people whom you will meet in the street or at parties or in church; people whom you will find difficult to look in the eye if you decline their application. That explains what I did with John and Mary. I declined, but I blamed my negative response on the bank's stringent, inflexible loan policy. I may even have used the word "unfair."

Loan applicants, no matter their circumstance, tend to view negative reactions from loan officers as a signal that the loan officer harbors personal animosity or simply is incompetent. The applicant's next inclination is to go over the loan officer's head and seek a hearing from his "more experienced and reasonable" superior. In my years of credit management, such a ploy worked many times—either by appealing to senior bank officers or, in the case of industrial credit, to owners of companies. Why? Because not everyone who lends money or extends credit applies the same principles to the process.

John and Mary found a more senior lending officer who had a relationship with John's parents. The new credit was extended, without asking that John's father personally guarantee or co-sign the loan. I only wish that the loan officer, and not me, had been the person sent five months later to accompany a collections employee to the Parsons home. Mission: repossess John's car and the couple's furniture. Careful readers will have noted that we carted away the furniture about the time that Mary was scheduled to bring home their new child.

When mother and child did leave the hospital, the Parsons house was nearly empty. It was decided that Mary and the baby would go to her mother's for a few weeks and spend some time with the proud grandparents. John's overtime, meanwhile, was cut back drastically. With Mary's income a thing of the past, and John's shrinking, the Parsons home was listed for sale.

About three years later, John and Mary crossed my path again when Mary—tugging two small children and pulling a baby stroller—reapplied for credit at Sears, where I was assistant credit manager. Amazingly, they had avoided filing bankruptcy. After obtaining a credit report, I could easily see why. They had made payment agreements with a number of creditors and had been struggling to get out of debt ever since I had last seen them. In truth, they were even further in debt.

In a case of debtor's *deja vu,* they once again appealed my denial—this time to a credit manager driven either by a strong desire to increase sales or, more likely, by one of those incessant contests to see which credit manager can put the most new accounts on the books.

I can assure you, from a credit manager's and collector's point of view, that there is a certain finality to a department store charge account. Repossessing shirts, socks or underwear (clothing makes up 90 percent of revolving credit sales) is not a very pragmatic proposition. Renewing John and Mary's account was not the smartest move in the long history of Sears & Roebuck. Their account, of course, became a continuing problem for the collection department.

The Parsonses also became a continuing astonishment to me—much as I suppose a psychologist is enthralled by his most exotic cases. From time to time I would see John drive through town in a brand-new car. I could only surmise how this perpetually bankrupt couple continued to live light years into their futures. There was a bit of jealousy in my bewilderment, as I was struggling with my own family finances at the time.

A chunk of the mystery unfolded through one of my first business consulting jobs, an automobile dealership that had greatly overextended its own credit capacity. Faced with declining volume, it was forced to sell cars—both new and used —to individuals with marginal credit, at best. When auto dealers are so desperate, the institutions that finance the sales require the dealer to sell "with recourse." That means when the bank repossesses the vehicle, it is delivered to the dealer—who then must write a check for the unpaid balance. With even more questionable debtors, the bank demands "full recourse and unconditional guarantee." That means the bank picks up the phone, tells the dealer to send the check and to go repossess the car himself.

Scanning through numerous pages of full recourse transactions at the auto dealer I was working with, I learned the reason John Parsons was able to sport around town with his brand-new wheels. The only faith and credit the bank had extended for John's vehicle was the cost of a phone call. A local call, at that.

Years later, my consulting firm established in the city and this remarkable couple from smalltown banking long since having passed from my life, I chanced across them yet again. I was consulting for a bank holding company that sought to acquire one of the local financial institutions. Suffice it to say that, in their early 50s, John and Mary were still managing to keep their noses barely above the quicksand. I will never know how.

Citing the Parsons affair in this book is not unlike writing a book on coronary health and citing the history of a family that has maintained, through three generations, an average weight of 300 pounds without suffering a single heart attack. The citation is not meant to be demonstrative, but awe-inspiring—an admission that every rule of probability can be broken on some random pass of the dice.

More constructively, this legendary couple—they are legendary to me, at least—do demonstrate the tandem treadmill on which couples are so amazingly willing to launch their lifetime marathon. If you recognize yourself in John and Mary's portrait, then I trust you already have perceived that you are not likely to run as far as they have. John and Mary are freaks. They have survived. Sometimes the reckoning comes very late in the game, however, and for John and Mary it is not yet over.

I suppose one or two physical freaks also exist, with naturally strong hearts and lungs and muscles, who can get up off the couch and run for 26 miles. Like John and Mary, they should charge admission.

True love, they say, conquers all. My personal belief is that true love is something achieved only after years of marriage, but that kind of judgment lies beyond my credentials. My professional and credentialed belief, which I hold with great certitude, is that young people who marry wearing financial blinders are at best an even-money bet for reaching a double-digit anniversary.

The worst possible circumstance—a bride and groom who are both buried in debt—is commonplace. The most common compounding of that circumstance—a bride and groom who do not sit down, lay the books on the table and plan accordingly—is also commonplace. Who wants to add up debts and balance them against income "when you," as the song says, "have romance on the menu"? It is worth noting that the song is *What a Difference a Day Made*. And does a day or two or 30 or 60 or 90 (and on into the billing cycle) *ever* make a difference!

A couple starts out in the hole with debts brought to the marriage. Expenses will rise (and income probably will fall) with the arrival of children. The marathon equation, if it ever was balanced, becomes increasingly shaky.

Bad habits in managing money and using credit remain hidden until warning lights flash (red-type SHUTOFF overprints on the utility bills). In the past, both husband and wife may have relied on parents as a safety valve when personal finances got out of line. Once married, they are reluctant even to discuss money problems with parents, and more so with in-laws. The smiling faces from the wedding pictures find themselves isolated in a losing equation. Heated arguments about money may futilely toss the blame back and forth, tending to leave the couple isolated not only from their old safety valves but even from each other.

In a picture that bleak, our sky-high divorce rates are not the least bit surprising. Finances alone would seem enough to do the job.

Money problems in a marriage are not necessarily, of course, present from the outset. But whether brought to the marriage or created after the wedding, a financial problem is a result of living today on tomorrow's money.

Complete frankness and a head-on approach to the problem are the only ways to solve it—for couples or singles, young or old. So much agony in any financial situation can be eliminated through early intervention.

In marriage, that means acting before the church and the reception hall are booked. One would think that prospective couples who are perfectly willing to settle issues such as names of unborn children, future vacation destinations, private time— and a host of ultrapersonal questions—would also be willing to take a detailed look at the marathon equation. It will, after all, decide whether any of these things are going to be realities or pipe dreams.

No marriage should take place on a bankruptcy budget. Period. Couples should prepare a complete list of all outstanding obligations. Short-term debt should be eliminated before the ceremony. Long-term debt should be reduced, by selling assets or by seeking parental assistance or by setting a later wedding date.

I hear that cry again: "Get real!" And once again I say that *this* is reality, evidenced by the fact that marriages fail more often than favorites win at the race track.

True love is indeed a wonderful thing. Try to give your marriage a financial basis to last a few years. Then you can discover what true love—the sharing of joys and sorrows in the crucible of time—is all about.

9

Crisis, Yes; Surprise, No

An earnest young man, bemoaning the state of the middle class, recently engaged me in conversation. "A family of four," he asserted, "can't sustain 'the American standard of living' even on take-home income of $750 a week."

I grant that "the American standard of living" is quite a hazy concept. If reality were defined as the designer living rooms and imported luxury sedans one sees in TV dramas and commercials, then my friend might have a point. He would also have a severe reality problem.

"You're putting the cart before the horse," I told him. Although guessing that his mythical couple were real people, and probably living in his house, I outlined a generic scenario. He nodded agreement through every step.

If husband and wife are making a combined net income of $750 a week, I told him, that's $39,000 a year—$3,250 a month. If a family of four is at that level without any debt, they ought to be able to live quite nicely.

The problem is, before getting to that level, they lived far into the future. Now their income is $3,250 a month, but they are living at $3,750 a month. A substantial sum, double the average annual income in some nations, moves through their checking account every month. Nonetheless, it often is an adventure for this couple to scrape up cash for orange juice and coffee.

"Exactly my point," he said, missing mine by a wide margin.

When I first considered writing a book, its scope was limited to helping individuals get through *financial crises*. But the more I reflected on what I've seen over the last three decades, the more I realized that the term "financial crisis"—though accurate—does not really do the job. That's when I consciously decided to go ahead and pepper these pages with "Living in the Future," a phrase I have long used conversationally. It may at first be taken as overdramatic and rhetorical, but I think many readers already comprehend the truth of it. We are talking about a way of life, not an arithmetic problem. My young friend's $750-a-week tale of woe helps to illustrate.

First, "crisis" suggests something that develops overnight. In a small minority of cases, natural disasters and such, that is true. Not so with Living in the Future, the cause of the all-American financial dilemma.

Two people who have been living together for seven or eight years don't suddenly say: "Boy, did we ever get ourselves buried in debt last month!" It has been a slow buildup, progressing from whatever financial discipline they had as a child, through their teenaged and young adult years, through the first years of their lives together. Quite possibly, with two children and a $3,250 monthly income, they are still paying for goods bought when they were childless. When you spend your future, you are reaching into a different, unknown set of circumstances. For example, those two tykes sleeping upstairs.

Whatever their circumstances—single or married, childless or not, high income or low, 20-something or 40-something—people who defy the marathon equation set the stage for disaster. One day, the victim might at last say to himself, in whatever words: "This a financial crisis." Yes, it is; but it has been percolating for a long, long time. His crisis is no greater today than it was six months ago. And getting his most vocal creditor off his back for a month or two will not end the crisis. Millions of Americans actually live in *perpetual* financial crisis. They participate not in a rat race but in an illusory balancing act. Entire subdivisions of illusionists teeter between their split-level castles and a trip to bankruptcy court. They *are already bankrupt.* Just as a murderer is a murderer whether or not he is ever found out and brought to trial, a bankrupt is a bankrupt whether or not he has the papers to prove it. Just as some bankrupt companies manage to continue in business with well-paid executives and corporate jets, bankrupt individuals manage to park their expensive cars at fine addresses and settle down for an evening of video on huge projection-screen TVs. Ask them what in the world they are doing, and the answer is likely to be: "Living the good life."

Living the mortgaged life would be closer to the truth. Like John and Mary Parsons, they just might carry it off for an incredibly long time. As long as you rob Peter to pay Paul, as long as you can squeeze a little cash flow from the nearest rock, you can keep the malevolent thing alive. It is also true that, as odds go, you have an excellent short-term shot at beating the house playing Russian roulette. Like the Christopher Walken character in *The Deer Hunter,* players of Living in the Future spin the cylinder, pull the trigger, and live on for another round.

So the typical "financial crisis" most definitely is not a problem that popped up just the other day.

Another serious fault with the phraseology is that "financial crisis" suggests something unusual, if not rare. The fact is, we all live in a world of debt and only a statistically insignificant number of us will get through our full measure of years without experiencing a financial crisis. It's a simple fact of life. What separates us into three meaningful groups is how we respond.

- A few Americans live too far into the future, confront the problem, extricate themselves and say: "No way am I ever going back there." This once-burned individual is sorely tempted by a stylish new car, but understands he can acquire it today only by assuming unrealistic debt. He is saved by a subconscious bell and an insistent voice that warns: "Dummy!" He likes toys as much as the next person but refuses to be sucker-punched by materialism.

- Many—maybe most—Americans drift in and out of serious financial problems. These individuals let their indebtedness career out of control to the farthest point where brakes can still be applied. Then, by living for a time significantly *less well* than their income would otherwise allow, they inch back from the precipice and avoid a fatal crash. Lacking discipline, however, they rev up the credit engine and court disaster yet again. It's like yo-yo dieting: short-term gain, short-term loss, short-term gain, short-term loss—adding up to long-term ill health. By now, there shouldn't be a person in America who doesn't understand that crash diets are meaningless. A permanent change of lifestyle is the only way to get fit and stay that way.
- Some Americans bury themselves in debt and spend a lifetime flailing away there, scarcely able to breathe. These are the perpetual players of Living in the Future. Can they have a happy day? Can they sleep? I don't see how. Perhaps it's in the genes.

The only conclusion I can reach is that debt is like alcohol. Used in moderation it can afford pleasure. You will even find a few experts whose studies say a small ration can be good for you. The bad news is that it can be addictive. The good news is that you can do something about the addiction, if someone shows you the way and if you respond with discipline.

Whether an alcohol crisis or a financial crisis, only one approach to a solution exists. That is to admit: "I have a problem." And then to meet it head-on.

Yes, you may have gotten into this financial situation by trying to provide the good life for your family. Yes, it's tough to make ends meet. And yes, perhaps the economy is bad. None of those factors can explain away the essential fact: *You have a financial problem.* It's not a passing headache. It's not going to disappear. It's a basic, acute, long-term situation.

Nasty words an alcoholic may have said to the boss's wife last night after the fifth martini are not the cause of his agony this morning. And that dunning phone call from the bank this morning is not the cause of a bankrupt consumer's agony this afternoon. The agony derives from prolonging the root cause, from continually denying that a problem exists.

Unfortunately, no Alcoholics Anonymous serves victims of Living in the Future. They must tough it out not only alone, but with a credit-crazed society dangling the addictive substance in their noses and urging them back to the trough. This is no exaggeration. Amazingly, if a victim reaches absolute rock bottom— if he becomes legally bankrupt—many creditors will be even more eager to pour him a drink. After all, the slate is clean and he has no debts!

Admitting a financial problem, then, is the all-important Step One; but solving the problem will require much more.

If you wish to be unburied, you must stop throwing dirt on your head. If you have a cold and wish to avoid pneumonia, you must not go out in the snow stark naked. If you wish not to bleed to death, you must stop the flow of blood. So Step Two is as simple and singular as Step One. There are no substitutions. The only way to solve a financial problem is to *stop Living in the Future*. Stop adding to your debt.

Step Two automatically leads to Step Three. This explains the reluctance of debtors to take any step at all, because Step Three requires you to *endure some pain*. You must bite the bullet to get the marathon equation back in balance. You must withdraw from the future and start living in the present.

This means you must surrender or buy back much of the future that you squandered at the credit window. Your income must do more than meet today's expenses. It also must attack that thing which is sucking your breath away—debt service. Time to start repaying both Peter and Paul. Explain to the world how that can be done without pain, and you will become a truly wealthy person.

Let's assume that you have done the courageous and necessary thing, which is to take Steps One and Two. As a financially troubled individual, Step Three presents you with exactly the same two options confronted by a financially troubled company. If your financial crisis amounts to nothing more than serious trouble, you can reorganize. Reorganization involves pain. If your financial crisis has escalated to full-blown disaster, with no hope of ever paying back your creditors, you can go to court and declare bankruptcy. Formal bankruptcy involves even more pain.

Let's further assume that reorganization is within your grasp. If it is not, this book can do little except to prepare you for the pain, assure you that you are not alone, inspire you to stay clean when the pain subsides (as it will), and, I hope, encourage you to re-examine your attitude toward Living in the Future.

If you are going to reorganize, you need a tool to dig yourself out: simple, unwavering, eyes-straight-on-the-target discipline. It is nice to be creative, but do not waste valuable breath scurrying about in search of shortcuts or brainstorms that would lead along an easier path. None exist. Like a troubled corporation, you are about to downsize. All the creativity in the world will not build you a 10-room house with six rooms of lumber.

With Step Two, you stopped acquiring debt. If you are fortunate, you have not gotten too far down the suicide path of acquiring debt to pay other debt. That will go a long way toward determining how many assets you must sell.

Do I mean you *must* get rid of assets?

Probably. Acquiring assets—many of which depreciated to a tiny fraction of their purchase price the moment you carted them home—was the principal way you got into this sad situation. Each mortgaged asset represents a chip or a chunk of your future, spent before its time.

If you have relatively few such assets, and if their debt service is low enough in relation to your income, you can keep them and work your way back into the present. With some pain. Otherwise, you'll have to let some assets go. With greater pain.

As an extreme but true example, some people live frugally and at the same time so far into the future as to defy belief. How can a couple live on bologna and white bread, clothe themselves at resale shops, stay home seven nights a week, never take a vacation and be a month behind on their house payment? It happens, more or less as described, all the time. This couple has focused their vision of the American standard of living, and their place in it, squarely on a house—and probably on the two cars in its garage. They shun the theater tickets and the fine clothes and all the baubles in the slick magazine ads; but to them being an American means a certain house in a certain place and, by God, they are Americans. Somehow, on $700 a week take-home income, they have gotten into a $1,400 per month mortgage. Maybe the banker was asleep at the closing. Maybe their income has fallen. But there they sit.

The house must go. They must trade down to a lesser dwelling, or rent an apartment. They must become a one-car family, if possible, or become a lesser-car family. Otherwise they will get so far into the future that they will be sitting on the curb with nothing to trade and no wheels in which to escape. The arithmetic already points them in that direction. A single major unexpected expense will take them there in a minute.

At the opposite extreme, a couple has been married for 20 years and in the same house for 16 years. Their take-home income is $800 a week. Because of longevity at one address in a blue-collar suburb, their mortgage is a blessedly low $450 a month—including taxes and insurance. After fully paying the cost of the roof over their heads, they have $3,000 and a pair of movie tickets left over every month. This couple will never be in the Social Register, but they clearly should be living somebody's version of the good life.

Instead, a jumbled pile of papers on a desk in an upstairs bedroom tells the woeful tale. Buried, and buried deep. Visa and MasterCard with a $5,000 line on each, and each nearly maximized. A thousand dollars owed to a local department store, 30 days late. Payment books for his six-month-old car and her year-old car and their teenager's five-year-old car (the boy is supposed to pay Mom and Dad in cash, but often skips a beat). Husband and wife both charge their *gasoline*, and that bill is in the pile. There are bills for magazine subscriptions and cable TV and the 60-days-same-as-cash compact disc player from the appliance store's spring sale. And on and on.

Not a single one of these purchases is outrageous, in itself.

It's their profusion, and the fact that this couple appears never to have paid cash for so much as an ice cream cone, that makes them a living, breathing all-American financial crisis. In fact, this couple's *interest payments on personal debt* will surpass average annual income in all but the most industrialized nations on Earth.

Fortunately for them, Step One and Step Two—plus living for a year or so as frugally as the house-poor couple in our first example—will be almost enough to draw back from the precipice and approach living in the present. Junior must either make those payments or lose his car. (He's on course to repeat this ugly scene in the next generation.) Mom and Dad might want to consider trading down to cheaper vehicles so as to extract a little walking-around money from the budget. Otherwise, resolve and discipline—and some pain—will suffice.

If this couple allows the current scenario to continue, however, they might achieve the incredible: losing a house when their *weekly* income nearly doubles their monthly payment.

Each of these two couples represents a fairly extreme example of Living in the Future, but each case resounds with familiarity. Each couple finds itself in a financial crisis, but it didn't "happen" yesterday. And I would suggest that there is nothing unusual, let alone rare, about the general facts of each case.

Those who are house-poor actually have served themselves a double-dose of Living in the Future. Not only are they saddled with a very large debt very far into the future, but every penny of it is gambled on the terribly shaky proposition that tomorrow will be better than today in *two* ways: (1) Income will rise so as to make payments reasonable, and (2) when the time comes to sell, by choice or necessity, the house will fetch *more* than the original purchase price.

Our second classic couple, who just can't say no with their plastic, simply must learn how to cope through discipline. Easy consumer credit and rock-and-roll arrived on the scene at virtually the same time. Both appear to be here to stay, but credit is the more universal language. Heavy metal and Andy Williams tapes both are chargeable at your local music outlet. Within the last year or two, it has become possible to buy broccoli with a VISA card at the grocery store. I'm not sure the screenwriter understood his prophetic powers when young Dustin Hoffman in *The Graduate* got an earful of the future: "It's *plastic!*"

How many Americans can see a piece of themselves reflected in one or both of these couples?

The more appropriate questions are:

• How many have been there but will never go back?
• How many drift in and out of that grim picture?
• How many are perpetually insolvent?

10

How Bad Is It?

It's a time of cold numbers and hot emotions. You have admitted a financial problem. You have stopped the bleeding by refusing to go further into debt. It's time to add and, mostly, subtract.

A financial problem can be solved only if you are truly dedicated to doing so, because usually it means a change in lifestyle. Restructuring finances commonly produces a period of acute embarrassment and a testing of some personal relationships. That's the down side. The up side—a new kind of self-esteem rooted in economic reality, a long-lost sense of being *in control*—more than compensates for the down.

The process tends to produce a V-shaped emotional curve.

Admitting the problem and finding the courage to tackle it creates an initial euphoria. For a moment, the process might even seem easy. It isn't.

Immersing yourself in the numerical facts of your situation and then taking hard, necessary steps can bring remorse and, at first, a sense of futility. If you ever have dieted to lose weight, you have had a glimpse of the discipline and time frame necessary to do the job. If your lifestyle downsizing is of serious proportion, you quite likely will lose or alter some personal relationships that have been based at least in part on phony materialism.

Finally, if you stick with *your plan,* you will discover that living within your economic reality has not ended your life. In fact, your life will have changed for the better. There will be a holistic effect, just as getting physically fit produces an overall positive effect that goes far beyond strengthening a few muscles.

Of course, that scenario is a stereotype, a generic snapshot. We are not cardboard cutouts. Our lives, in terms of both personal finance and personal relationships, are unique. All I can say is that I have watched this scenario played out so many times, in so many contexts, that I feel at least as confident in the prescription as I would in recommending aspirin for a headache.

The first priority is to find out just how much trouble you are in. Shutoff notices and red ink and dunning phone calls usually let an individual know he or she has a serious problem. Seldom, however, can the financially troubled person give an accurate description of the trouble's magnitude. From time to time they pick up a stack of bills and write checks until the account is empty (hopefully no further). The remaining bills are then shoved back into the pile. This individual's specific financial self-knowledge extends no further than being able, perhaps, to tell you his checkbook balance.

That little scenario, by the way, may sound decidedly blue-collar. Let me assure you that the bill-shuffling syndrome accurately describes the financial life of many individuals who earn salaries *far* above the median. It even accurately describes the accounts payable department of thousands of troubled companies.

So as an individual resolutely stepping toward financial recovery, what you are about to do will put you light years ahead of hundreds of thousands—millions?—of your fellow Americans. You are going to prepare a Debt Magnitude Analysis.

If you are single, this task—and all the decisions that flow from it—are yours alone. If you are married, you should not have gotten this far without drawing your spouse into the process. Regardless of which partner contributed most to creating the problem, the responsibility for solving it must be shared. It is even a good idea to draw older children into the process, and let them learn by sharing in the problem-solving.

Analyzing how far you are buried in debt requires total honesty. Every single obligation—regardless of size, to whom it is owed, or its nature—must be included in a comprehensive and accurate list. This includes debts to relatives, friends and associates, and commitments to religious and charitable institutions. In your mind, these obligations may not be in the same class as a two-month-old water bill; but when you walk into church, or when you meet your creditor friend at a party, the obligations will be real. Assuming you plan to pay them, they will be a crack in the financial dike you are trying to build. List *everything*.

Make a series of vertical columns across a wide page. You can format your Debt Magnitude Analysis just as the mythical Bill Dunn has analyzed his own sad situation, on Page 81. You'll meet young Mr. Dunn shortly.

Column one names the *creditor*. Remember, for our purposes here, an entry might be the largest bank in Manhattan or it might be a favorite aunt.

Column two states the *nature of debt:* automobile loan, insurance, personal loan, etc. If you enter a preponderance of "charge account" entries here, you already have a handle on where your problem originated.

Column three lists the *total of debt* for each entry. It is important to list total debt even for obligations, such as car loans or leases, in which you normally think in terms of monthly payments.

Column four lists the *term* of all obligations, where appropriate—such as the number of months remaining on a car loan, or "revolving" for a department store charge, or "annual" for an insurance premium.

Column five lists the amount for each *single-payment* obligation. These could be cash personal loans or a doctor's bill—any one-time payment due.

Column six lists *monthly payments*. Record all monthly obligations, using an average for revolving charges. When you have completely and honestly listed every financial obligation in your household, compute totals at the bottom of columns three, five and six.

BILL DUNN'S DEBT MAGNITUDE ANALYSIS

Creditor	Nature of Debt	Outstanding Debt Total	Remaining in Term	Single Payment	Monthly Payment
Local Bank	Automobile Loan	13,739.76*	27 Months		508.88
Department Store	Charge Account	1,746.00	Revolving		461.00
Natl. Charge Card	Charge Account	1,800.00	Revolving		180.00
Natl. Charge Card	Charge Account	1,675.00	Revolving		168.00
Credit Union	Loan	1,500.00	Revolving		150.00
Doctor	Service	350.00		350.00	
Dentist	Service	275.00		275.00	
Clinic	Service	150.00		150.00	
Neighbor	Loan	250.00		250.00	
Parents	Loan	4,000.00	40 Months		100.00
Electricity	Service	75.00			75.00
Telephone	Service	55.00			55.00
Gas	Service	50.00			50.00
Cable TV	Service	30.00			30.00
Auto Insurance	Coverage	800.00	8 Months		100.00
Apartment	Lease	5,500.00	10 Months		550.00
Health Club (Gym)	Service	50.00			50.00
Magazines	Subscriptions	65.00		65.00	
Church Pledge	Account	500.00	5 months		100.00
		32,610.76		1,090.00	2,577.98

* Includes interest; principal is $12,393.96

It may not be a pretty picture that you are developing, but it is a useful one. Think of it as an X ray of your fractured finances. You are the doctor, and the X ray will be crucial to deciding the appropriate course of care: aspirin, radical surgery, or something in between.

The marathon equation is simple. However, the degree to which you have allowed the equation to become unbalanced and the speed with which you have recognized a problem and acted on it, along with numerous less important factors, allow for a broad range of diagnoses.

Somewhere out there, for example, still dwell a good many people who are terrified by a past-due notice. Such an individual might declare a financial crisis and take a serious look at his personal books so early that not much is required but common-sense belt-tightening. This person likely will have arrived at a sound diagnosis and course of care, and will have achieved some personal insight, an instant after looking at his debt X ray.

Another person might have a single anchor around his or her neck, an overwhelming obligation that hopelessly skews the equation. If it is a discretionary anchor—remember, honesty is required—then this exercise is a no-brainer. It can be a toy, such as a 40-foot boat. It can be a house, because a house beyond your means *is* discretionary. It can be a hobby, such as membership in a hunt club (chasing the foxes and maintaining a horse, or shooting deer and maintaining a 4X4 vehicle; either one will do it). Whatever this discretionary anchor, it must be cut loose. If it is tragically non-discretionary, such as care for an invalid relative, I can offer nothing but the scant comfort in knowing that most people with troubled finances do not have such noble motives.

Let us assume, however, that the most cursory study of your Debt Magnitude Analysis reveals that you are in a more typical nose dive, weighed down by numerous ill-entered obligations, with terra firma rapidly approaching. Chopping the entertainment budget, skipping a vacation trip and forgoing new clothes for a few months will not begin to solve your problem.

You have been seriously Living in the Future, and you

must do a serious restructuring of your finances to regain the present. Parts of your situation might bear a resemblance to the troublesome X ray of our mythical Bill Dunn. Let's take a look at his Debt Magnitude Analysis on Page 81 and see what we can learn from six stark columns.

Bill is 27 and single, an apartment-dweller who—as you can see at a glance—has dipped far into his future on numerous fronts.

You need to know that Bill's gross after-tax income is $2,600 a month, or $600 a week, a respectable sum for a young man in the current job market. But for most of his adulthood he has churned a healthy percentage of it in what would be called the entertainment portion of his budget, if he had a budget. And he has assumed debt which—viewed from any angle—is wildly unrealistic.

At 27, with not even spousal obligations, let alone children, and with no home mortgage, his total debt ($32,610.76) exceeds his annual take-home pay ($31,200). Should he marry, he will bring a time bomb to the altar.

It's easy to see why Bill finally has gotten around to admitting a problem and analyzing his debt. Things have gotten so far out of hand that his finances are about to melt down like an overheated nuclear reactor. So many fuel rods (debt transactions) have been inserted that the most adroit credit technician could not prevent disaster any longer.

Monthly payments on his debt total $2,577.98! That means that putting food on his table; fueling and maintaining his car; entertaining himself, and perhaps a girlfriend; buying the occasional pair of socks and underwear; paying for any unforeseen expenses, emergency or otherwise—all would have to be achieved on exactly $22.02 a month.

You say *nobody* could get into such a mess? Wrong. It's not even near being a worst-case scenario. In fact, we're going to use the Debt Magnitude Analysis and a restructuring plan to help pull Bill out of his crisis. He will not need to declare bankruptcy. And we will make him *virtually debt-free,* in less than a year.

First, let's get the full flavor of how Bill did the seemingly impossible and got where he is. You may wish to refer to his analysis chart as we go along.

Bill has $2,000 credit limits at a department store and on two national charge cards. All three are near-maximized.

He has an auto loan, with 27 of 36 payments remaining.

He dipped into his credit union for another loan because, even though he knew he was insolvent, it seemed that after putting in a hard year on the job he deserved a genuine vacation, via commercial aviation, to a hotel in a warm climate.

Bill has the usual collection of utility and medical bills outstanding. He also is a religious young man, and has pledged $100 a month for the next five months to his church.

Having a sizeable amount of credit at his disposal, and having used it unwisely, Bill decided 10 months ago to turn to his parents for a $4,000 interest-free loan that would "put his finances in order."

At almost the same time, and unfortunately for Mom and Dad, the data services company where Bill works was swamped with new clients. Bill went on a six-day week and, suddenly, the cash flow improved considerably. With Mom and Dad's approval—but without their real understanding of just how far their son was Living in the Future—Bill paid down only a few bills with their loan, and used $2,000 of it for a down payment on an $18,000 car.

Several months later, Bill's employer lost a major client and put him back on a 40-hour week. Two weeks after that, Bill's best friend left town for greener pastures in Texas. Not only did Bill lose a good friend, he lost the roommate who had been paying half the rent. Already overextended, Bill's position suddenly became hopeless.

Since then, Bill has been deep into the bill-shuffling syndrome.

The substantial loan from his parents has never—as we said at the finance company 30 years ago—"left the post:" Not a single penny has been paid. And all three of his medical bills are at least second notice.

Fun-loving Bill lately has been living like a hermit, but

inevitably sinking nonetheless. He sold a motorcycle, picking up a couple of months' living expenses. Last month he got by after turning to a neighbor for $250 (which you see on the Debt Magnitude Analysis, and which by falling overdue has inspired Bill to address his problem). He even, once or twice a month, unconsciously has been picking up $25 by sleeping in on Sunday (he thinks of his church pledge as $25 in the plate each time he attends service).

Bill has no yacht, no single overwhelmingly unrealistic mortgaged asset to discard and lighten the load. And he has buried himself too deep to extract himself simply by cutting back on the entertainment. In fact, he already has done that.

That's what adding up the numbers reveals.

Now it's time for Bill to subtract—to construct a plan, and to restructure.

11

Restructuring

With your debt analyzed, you understand your problem in painful detail. And you recall that all the high-priced financial advice in the world can give you just three options: increase cash flow, or lower expenses, or do both.

The first option—adding muscle to the positive side of the marathon equation—isn't available to most of us. Even if it is available, it's not necessarily the best option.

If, for example, you are self-employed or are a commissioned salesperson, then perhaps you've been coasting lately. If so, you obviously can and must increase your cash flow by working harder. Almost certainly, however, you'll also need to lower expenses.

If your health, constitution, the job market and the parameters of your current position allow it, you can earn a second income. Hard work cures many ills. There is a limit, however, to what personal health and family relationships can handle.

You can, of course, get a raise, or get a better job. Or can you?

All of these paycheck possibilities—even if practical—seldom can overtake the lifestyle that got you in trouble in the first place.

Another way of adding weight to the positive side of the

marathon equation is to solve your problem by dipping, yet again, into the future. That is, to borrow money—preferably from an interest-free angel—and pay your bills.

Interest-free or not, a loan by itself will not solve a thing. It offers a single, manageable payment extended over a period that, in effect, turns all of your short-term debt into long-term debt. In theory, that is an acceptable solution. But without a change in lifestyle, the loan "solution" offers not much more than an opportunity to make the problem much worse. And, of course, there is the matter of being able to find such a loan.

So all signs in a financial crisis—barring something which you can do nothing about, namely outrageous good luck—point to the second option. You must adopt a lifestyle that is consistent with your current economic reality.

From this point forward, your steps will be in every respect analogous to those of a troubled company seeking to reorganize *its* finances without entering the courtroom.

You are going to disappoint certain people, most especially your creditors, a great deal. But as long as you are faithful to your plan, everyone—including your creditors—will emerge from this mess with the best possible outcome. They will get their money, though not nearly as quickly as had been promised. You will retain your integrity and self-esteem for having fulfilled your obligations, and your marathon equation will be back in balance. Chances are good that the lesson will stick, and your financial fitness will not soon return to flab.

Your debt has been analyzed. Not much income analysis is required, if you are like most people. Your income is fixed, more or less, and you should have no trouble projecting cash flow for the next 30 days. This is important, because it is within the first 30 days of restructuring that you will fail or succeed. If you fail, you must return to square one and develop a new plan. Each time you do, your chances of success diminish.

First, you institute "the freeze."

For the next 30 days—or even 60 days, if necessary—the only payments you will make will be your utility and rent or mortgage payments, insurance coverage that otherwise will lapse, a reasonable allotment for food, and necessary transportation costs. All other income is designated for a cash reserve as you develop your restructuring plan.

This cash reserve does *not* mean that you suddenly have a new discretionary cash flow in which to dip. This is a sacred cookie jar. Get your hand caught in it, and your best-laid plan will disintegrate.

Make immediate personal contact with all of your local creditors. Contact out-of-town creditors by mail. Whether in person or by mail, all creditors should receive a letter informing them that you have a serious financial problem and are working on the solution. Request that charge accounts be closed immediately, and return all charge cards. Request a 30-day moratorium on all payments until you are able to present creditors with a repayment plan for their approval. Keep copies of all letters for your files.

I never said it would be easy.

If you have a national charge card with a significant line of credit unused, you will be tempted to continue making minimum payments while holding the card in reserve for emergencies—such as a flight to a sick relative's bedside, or to repair a vehicle necessary for transportation to work. If you can honestly assert that you will not retrigger the whole vicious cycle, you might consider keeping one such card. I wouldn't.

As you hammer out details of your restructuring plan, there *is* room for creativity. Priorities must be set, and options chosen.

To illustrate, let's return to the mythical case of Bill Dunn, and his Debt Magnitude Analysis on Page 81. Following Bill through his restructuring, step by step, requires some close attention. I think you'll find it illuminating, however, even if you are not actually going through the pain of a restructuring yourself. If you *are* restructuring, or if you want to get new insight on what a personal budget can mean, it is vital that you understand every move Bill makes.

Bill has taken the steps outlined above. Creditors have been notified, his plastic has been discarded, the freeze is in effect, and a plan must be drawn up.

From his monthly take-home income of $2,600, he must first pay necessities: $550 rent and $210 utilities (including cable TV). He must also set aside $60 for gasoline, and a food budget of $600 to get through the first 30 days. That leaves $1,180, less than half his take-home pay. It does not take a CPA to see that for Bill to amortize his debt in $2^{1}/_{2}$ years would take the devotion of a monk—even without the shiny new car that Bill so desperately wants to keep.

First, he looks for quick economies that could be made in his monthly debt service. He could, for example, reduce his monthly nut by $30 if he dropped cable TV service (which includes $12 for premium channels). But he thinks that, with his reduced lifestyle, cable will help him stay the course. He could sell his car, buy a transportation special with the meager profit, and have no monthly payment. But he points out that he would still need insurance and gasoline—and probably would incur serious repair bills. He could approach his parents about a moratorium on their loan (a moratorium he already has imposed unilaterally). But he has experienced nagging guilt on this one for months, and he wants to start paying Mom and Dad.

From the 19 items listed in his debt analysis, Bill can erase just one item without blinking—his monthly gym dues. He doesn't get to the club half as often as he intends, and he can turn to jogging for fitness. Small progress: Bill deducts $50 a month from his recurring payments. That puts his monthly take-home pay at a pathetic $72.02 above his debt analysis obligations.

Back to the drawing board. This is precisely the point in restructuring where options must be chosen, and where you can be somewhat creative.

- Option One: Bill has learned that he can get rid of his new car and buy "basic, second-hand transportation" that will be debt-free. There is some risk in that. But his monthly nut would decrease immediately by $508.88 (plus a $50 decrease in monthly insurance premium).
- Option Two: Dear old Mom and Dad. They probably are not eager to spend an evening closely examining young

Bill's books. But he could lay his carefully prepared plan on the table, and explain how at some date certain he will be free of debt, and would then begin to repay them.

- Option Three: This bachelor lifestyle is truly grand, but he could move out of his suburban studio and share a gentrified city flat with a friend from the office. There is the hassle of a sublease on the current place, but it could be done—for a saving of perhaps $300 a month.
- Option Four: At Bill's age, a second job does no favors to the social schedule. On the other hand, he has the health and energy to handle it. Newly armed with a budget and a sound sense of his financial reality, every hour on the job would be meaningful. Bill is a golfer, and his cousin has offered him a busy Saturday shift behind the counter at his pro shop. A potential $250-a-month boost to the picture.
- Option Five: Any combination of the above.

As Bill can see already, his situation is grim but far from hopeless. Many people must restructure from a point even deeper into the future. Many who are less buried still need restructuring.

Bill decides to draw up a plan relying on Option One (goodbye, car) and Option Four (hello, pro shop) to start moving the equation back toward equilibrium. Feeling that he already has stiffed his parents, he will invoke Option Two only if failure appears imminent. Nonetheless, he will have that session with Mom and Dad to show them what he is doing, finally, to "put his finances in order." He treasures his apartment even more than his car, so he will also try to avoid Option Three.

Now Bill draws out another sheet of paper and sorts out all of his debts as short-term, long-term and recurring. These no longer include his dear, departed car or his membership in the health club. His auto insurance has decreased to $50 a month because he is now driving a transportation special. He enters all these figures into three columns:

Short-Term		Long-Term		Recurring (Monthly)	
Doctor	$350	Dept. Store	$1,746	Electricity	$75
Dentist	275	Charge Card	1,800	Phone	55
Clinic	150	Charge Card	1,675	Utility Gas	50
Neighbor	250	Credit Union	1,500	Cable TV	30
Magazines	65	Parents	4,000	Car Policy	50
Final Gym Fee	50	Church	500	Apartment	550
	$1,140		$11,221		$810

Everything falls nicely into one of the three categories except Bill's church pledge. With some trepidation, he puts the pledge under "long term," knowing that these debts will be the last ones paid. He vows that during his restructuring plan he will also drop any spare change into the church collection plate.

Bill is very nearly ready to get to the heart of his plan. All that is lacking is a realistic accounting of what it will take "to live" while he unburies himself from debt. "Realistic" carries two important meanings here, whether you are putting together a restructuring plan or merely drawing up an honest budget to make sure that you never *need* a restructuring plan:

(1) Any plan, and any budget, must not be so spartan that it collapses the first time your car needs an oil change, or when you discover that your only winter coat is so threadbare that your boss will wonder if your generous salary is being spent on booze or illicit drugs. Food, clothing, shelter and transportation all must be taken care of before debt service.

(2) The amounts that you set aside to cover these necessities must indeed be *reasonable*. One cannot, for example, be living in expensive quarters and driving a Mercedes while asking the corner hardware store to restructure the payments on one's lawn mower. The legal and moral principles are obvious. Besides which, the whole idea is to get this debt monkey off your back as rapidly as possible. Living a lifestyle beyond your means has put you in trouble; it certainly won't bail you out.

Now, back to Bill Dunn.

He needs to include, under recurring expenses, the cost of operating and maintaining his second-hand car. And, though his department store debt clearly shows that his closet is not empty, he will need some kind of clothing allowance—because he will not charge so much as a pair of socks during his restructuring plan. (In budgeting any item, of course, multiply a weekly expense by 4 or divide an annual expense by 12 to arrive at a monthly estimate.)

So Bill's recurring payments now look like this:

Recurring (Monthly)	
Electricity	$75
Phone	55
Utility Gas	50
Cable TV	30
Car Insurance	50
Gasoline, Upkeep	120
Apartment	550
Clothing	50
Food	600
	$1,580

Bill now can see what blissful shape he would be in had he not taken on so much debt. His restructuring plan covers food, clothing, shelter, utilities and transportation—though clothing and transportation are at a reduced standard—and leaves $1,020 monthly cash reserve from his $2,600 take-home pay—plus the $250 a month he will make at the pro shop. That's $1,270 a month toward digging out!

The bad news is that he will have to devote nearly all this cash to debt service. The good news is that he will be in a very nice position after his plan has run its course.

The short-term and long-term debt that Bill is about to restructure add up to $12,361. On the one hand he is in varying degrees embarrassed, chagrined, humiliated, shamed and frustrated. On the other hand, he is near salivating at the impending freedom his calculations reveal. In less than a year he can be debt-free—including the $4,000 desperation loan on which he has never paid a cent!

He proceeds with a principle that applies to any restructuring plan, and that is to rid himself immediately of the entire column of short-term debt. It amounts to $1,140, and he can wipe it out during the 30-day freeze. Gone are the medical bills, the $250 debt that makes him embarrassed to pass his neighbor in the hall, his magazine bills and his final health club bill. He actually will have $130 left in his cash reserve at the end of the month.

Assuming you are making an honest budget, and are not providing yourself with unreasonable creature comforts, there is nothing wrong with maintaining a discreet and prudent amount of cash on hand within your plan. You must be able to put a new carburetor on that car if it breaks down. You must be able to see a weekly movie or otherwise reasonably entertain yourself to maintain your good humor and humanity. You must *not* dip into funds budgeted for debt service, so a certain amount of cash on hand is in fact *necessary*.

Under these circumstances, of course, you should not be *saving* money when interest-bearing debt remains to be paid. Every cent you earn on the savings will be more than devoured by interest on the unpaid debt.

Bill decides that after the 30-day freeze he will devote $1,020 a month to long-term debt service—meaning he is depending on his Saturday job for every penny of surplus cash. If the pro shop turns sour, he will have to moonlight elsewhere.

His next step is to determine how much of the $1,020 he will send to each long-term creditor. The formula is simple. Bill knows from his debt analysis that he has $11,221 to be repaid. He calculates that his department store balance comprises 16 percent of the total debt. So he would send them 16 percent of the $1,020, or $163.20. I say "would" because Bill has a special situation here with dear old Mom and Dad. Putting their $4,000 loan into the formula would actually pay them off *ahead* of time. That's not proper, so he decides to pay them $150 a month (he's 10 months behind on their payments) and to figure the other creditors' payments from the $870 that remains each month. That would make the department store's share 24 percent.

Here's what the arithmetic boils down to:

Creditor	Payment	
Department Store	$208.80	(24% of $870 debt service)
Natl. Charge Card	217.50	(25%)
Natl. Charge Card	200.00	(23%)
Credit Union	182.70	(21%)
Church	61.00	(7%)
	$870.00	100%

Add the $150 for Mom and Dad and you have reached the magic $1,020 figure.

None of these creditors will be happy, of course. That is particularly true of the department store, where more conservative revolving terms leave Bill's proposed payment far below the minimum (but only for a few months). The church pledge falls $39 short each month, but if all goes well at the pro shop, Reverend Smith will never know.

Now, look back to where Bill stood about 20 minutes and two chapters ago.

His monthly bills were pennies short of equalling his entire income! He faced a desperate situation. But he faced up to it, withdrew to a lifestyle that was within his means (below his means, actually, because he must pay for Living in the Future), and formulated a viable plan to balance the marathon equation.

All of his long-term debt, except the loan to his parents, will be paid off approximately *36 weeks* after the freeze. At that time, he will owe Mom and Dad just $2,650—and his cash flow will increase substantially. You are looking at a young man who, should he choose to do so, can move from utter disaster to total debt freedom in one year.

It would be a mistake to say that he accomplished all this simply by giving up a new car, working on Saturdays and adapting some austere spending habits for awhile. Yes, he did those things, and that's what made the numbers work. But more importantly he analyzed his situation and got in touch with his economic reality. That added dimension is the difference between giving up a fat-laden diet because it's this week's fad to do so and giving up a fat-laden diet because you have educated yourself to understand what a fatty diet does to the body over time. Young Bill is now fiscally fit, and in a position to stay that way.

This is such a simple prescription, but it is exactly what is done in the restructuring of a major corporation.

You analyze a troubled company's debt and find out what its income is going to be. You get the small creditors off the company's back. You see that the company's income will be down 50 percent this year, and you say, "That's your problem, and that means your expenses must go down dramatically. You might have needed 400 people last year, but this year 200 people will have to go. You might have needed 10 plants, but guess what's going to happen to five of them? You're going to shrink."

Then, after the 200 people have been dismissed and five plants have been closed, you sit down with the major creditors in a position to show that you mean business about straightening things out. You tell them, "This is what's available to you to work with."

You lower expenses or you increase income or you do both.

It always involves pain. In the case of a troubled company, the pain is shared by workers who lose their jobs. In the case of a troubled individual, he and his family bear the brunt of the pain.

This is what Bill Dunn did with his personal finances. It is a responsible person's way of resolving a serious financial problem. He avoided bankruptcy, and he charted a new course for his financial life. He made some creditors unhappy, but the worst thing that could happen to him is perhaps the best thing that could happen to him: He could lose his ability to use credit.

12

A Crisis for Every Age

All the things we might do with our income—live on it, save it, squander it, increase it, lose it on speculation or, like Bill Dunn, not be quite sure *what* we do with it—are *behaviors*. As such, they are subject to the usual run of childhood influences, teenage aberrations, adult addictions and corrective modifications. "Good habits and bad habits" is a simpler way of putting it.

Like any other behavior, our financial habits are shaped young and swayed by experience throughout the life cycle. Because our financial personality impacts so heavily on our security and happiness in later life, parents and teachers ought to grant it equal priority with, say, sex education or gym. Unfortunately, a youngster is more likely to get close instruction in remembering the capital of Idaho than he is in how to make and follow a budget.

Perhaps someone has done the research to show what percentage of financially troubled adults totally lacked financial discipline or meaningful financial education in their younger years. If so, I am unaware of it. Common sense suggests the percentage is high. I learned years ago never to bet. It's a serious temptation, however, to wager the farm that John and Mary Parsons were spending with both fists by the time they were 12, and that no one ever made an orderly effort to steer them straight.

We march through the life cycle tempted by numerous and various excesses or outright misbehaviors. The menu changes a bit with each phase of life. You need not be a behavioral scientist to observe, and to offer some insight. It should be no surprise that in 30-plus years of observing the human condition from a unique perspective, I can see the seeds of financial crisis every step of the way.

With absolutely no apology for a lack of scientific method, let me suggest that 10 phases of life—familiar to us all but seldom, if ever, examined as *financial* phases—comprise a sort of road map to Living in the Future. Maybe the educators and behaviorists will recognize the importance of financial personality and development, stick a few financial bytes in their databases, and get serious about making this marathon a part of our kids' basic curriculum.

I: The Age of Reason (or Unreason) Begins

It seems the psychologists can trace virtually every aspect of our adult behavior beyond our memories, into the crib, or even into the womb. How about stopping to think that the toddlers, grade-schoolers and pre-teens who get an unearned allowance on Friday and are broke on Saturday will, in a decade or two, be writing bad checks in the U.S. House or managing your bank's real estate portfolio?

No one can quarrel with the shrinks on the importance of childhood to adulthood. It is, in fact, one of those obvious but apparently difficult truths like the marathon equation or the three options in a financial crisis. Otherwise, every child would get some systematic instruction in working hard and well for his or her money, in delaying the gratification that money can buy, in saving for emergencies and major purchases.

Not every child will become a politician, lawyer or business executive. Every single one of them, however, will become a consumer. Think about it.

II: The Wild, Wild Teenaged Years

Any parent who has gone through the teenaged years with an offspring knows the importance of communication during the pre-teen years. There comes a time somewhere in puberty, and of varying duration, when you might have the most profound message to tell your son or daughter but you will be talking to *air*.

Your teen's financial life will be folded into his social life. And that means the herd instinct will stampede over all but the best-laid financial groundwork. You can ponder for months about how it can be possible that a certain name stitched on the pocket of a pair of denim pants can mean social life or death, but you will not change that fact.

The great temptation for frustrated parents here is to walk away from a seemingly hopeless situation. "We all do dumb things as teenagers," we say. Well, yes; but some of these things go beyond dumb, and will affect a young person for the rest of his life. Alcohol abuse and credit abuse, for example.

In today's society, "A penny saved is a penny earned" does not have quite the resonance of "Just say no." But, assuming that your child is successfully running the gauntlet of '90s horrors, you can do him no greater favor than steering him away from a life of perpetual financial crisis.

III: Young Love

This is the age of the singles scene, of a heightened sense that everything important in life comes off a car dealer's showroom floor or a department store clothes rack. It's also an age when appetite rages at a level far above income, but when full-time jobs nonetheless make charge cards possible. It's an age, therefore, of setting a gasoline can next to the stove.

In my youth, this soon led to the "Promise Her Anything" phase. In modern times, it more often leads to "The Co-op Deal" —two significant others sharing a roof but quite possibly forging ahead with separate and shaky financial agendas.

You will recall "Till Debt Do Us Part," and how Bill Dunn managed to bury himself without a single shared obligation. Young love is blind, and what it has most trouble seeing is numbers.

IV: The Early Married Years

Traditionally, of course, wedded bliss is launched on a sea of parental largesse and well-wishers' dinnerware. The ideal couple survives ceremony, reception, honeymoon and move-in without signing a single credit voucher. Good luck! More likely some mortgaging is involved, along with a honeymoon spending binge.

The euphoria of a new life together helps ensure that the newlyweds do everything financially possible to make it a short life together. They overdose on new debt, first to get "a place" and then to fill it up. Their future is so large, and is bound to be better financially than today, right?

Whatever material possessions a couple has on their first anniversary, odds are good that a great many of them have been purchased with a chunk of their future—which is unknown, and subject to radical change.

V: "Sweetheart, Guess What?"

This event always has been a financial jolt to young marrieds. Today—when the mother-to-be probably is a significant contributor to household income—it is more like an earthquake. The marathon equation stands on its head: expenses go up, and income goes down. If the equation was already unbalanced, the potential for tragedy is enormous.

Society now recognizes the terrible extent of child abuse in its various ugly forms. The causes are many and complicated, but surely the tension and resentment of financial crisis—for which this phase of life is tailor-made—must be a significant contributor. Just one more example of why finance should not be segregated from "more human" elements in the life experience.

This is often the life phase when we finally discover that we have no budget, that we have been improvising somewhere to the left of our financial reality. It is often the time when we first admit that we have "a financial crisis." If so, and if properly attacked, it can be the time when a marriage settles in for the long haul.

VI: Financing a Family

With additional mouths to feed, we enter a life phase longer than any yet encountered. That's why quality of life here depends so heavily on how we have organized our finances. It can be a long, tedious, frightening run of serious Living in the Future; or it can be a realistic period of goal-setting and child-rearing.

The latter, of course, includes heavy responsibility on the parents' part to prepare their children for running this same marathon. Remember that your own running style likely will be repeated in the next generation.

VII: The Kids Leave

Sometimes this means that parents can catch their financial breath. If, for example, your son signs a contract with the New York Mets. Otherwise—meaning almost all the time—the children are in college, and need support; or they are experiencing the various crises of newlyweds, and need help if you can give it.

The options here range from "Goodbye and good luck" to "Here's a bank card." Parental philosophy and financial ability assume greater weight than ever before. All that is certain is that out of the house seldom means out of need.

This often is a time when parents look ahead with great fondness to downsizing, to abandoning the four-bedroom barn for a condo or apartment or bungalow. That's an ever-less-likely dream (see VIII).

VIII: The Kids Come Back

Well, not *everybody* will endure this phase. But it becomes more commonplace with each passing year. The cliche of the '90s seems to be the Ph.D offspring living in the basement and working at McDonald's.

Kids come back for many reasons.

The college degree might not open any of the doors it was intended to open. Entry-level income and the cost of living might not be a very good match. The marriage that showed so much promise just a couple of years ago may be a thing of the past today.

In any of these cases, the kids might not only return—but they might bring others with them! The four-bedroom barn might be more taxed than ever.

Whether the kids' potential return is literal, or merely financial, it must be kept in mind.

IX: Pre-Retirement Years

Whether we get this far in the marathon with 10 children or none, affluent or barely making it, finances in order or in a mess, there comes a time when we realize—not in the very celebratory sense that it usually is stated—that "this is as good as it gets." We are not going to make $50,000 a year, or $100,000 a year, or $300,000 a year, or whatever that elusive goal was. We accept our financial status, realize that only one life phase remains ahead of us, and we try to get ready for it.

X: Senior Citizenship

The merry-go-round stops here. The most avid players of Living in the Future discover there is not much future left, and t is damned difficult to mortgage.

Interestingly, the very concept of "retirement"—of sitting back and enjoying this final phase—pretty much comes down to a question of debt service. By shuffling Social Security, a pension plan, investments or savings, or an avocational part-time job, most Americans can more or less accomplish a "good" retirement IF they do not bring debt to the equation.

Otherwise, death itself becomes nature's way of filing bankruptcy.

13

Today's Bike, Tomorrow's Convertible

Any parent who doesn't understand that peer pressure reaches down into the earliest ages simply has his head in the sand. "Keeping up with the Joneses" begins by keeping up with the toddler next door who just came home with a high-tech toy.

If you observe an adult who can't suppress a consumerist urge to "have it at all costs," you will describe his behavior as "child-like." It's not just a phrase. Fortunately, parents have at least a dozen years, before their offspring are drawn to the black hole of teenaged values, to plant some seeds of financial health.

We are born curiosity-seekers, soon discovering that light is something that comes and goes, that there are feet down at the end of our body, that there are other people in the world. The age of reason—the true point at which innocence is lost—is marked by our discovery that other people, other little people, have *things,* such as toys and dolls.

Where do these things come from? Well, Mom and Dad provide them. And now Mom and Dad have their first opportunities to be a hero or a villain in the eyes of their budding little consumer. That one I leave to the psychologists, the parenting experts, and the great common sense of thoughtful mothers and fathers. Suffice it to say that one of the great truths of life is that you *can't* have it all, you *never* can, and if you could, you would be very unhappy.

For our purposes, the lessons of Living in the Future begin when a child ascends to consumer status. That is, when he starts handling money and making his own purchases.

There are basically three lessons to be taught, and the first one is simple. All three, however, are ignored in too many homes:

- Money is something that comes from work, usually hard work.
- It must be spent wisely, which is both an art and a science.
- Some level of saving is a necessity, not a luxury.

A youngster's first cash flows from his parents. He will want to buy a host of items, from candy bars to movie tickets to Christmas presents, before he is capable of presenting himself to even the friendliest neighbor as a potential employee. Hence, the tradition our society has come to call an "allowance."

The connection between labor and cash, like every principle of personal finance, can be learned early with a little pain, or later with a great deal of pain. Applying the work/reward lesson starting from Day One of the allowance is almost a no-brainer. How this lesson ever can be botched is a total mystery, given its obviousness and the fact that there is no household without work to be done. To a child, the first allowance—no matter how small—has all the allure that his first full-time paycheck will have years down the road. So he is motivated to learn. Furthermore, if firmly shown that housework is a prerequisite for cash, a child has just two options: Make the connection or make no money.

Giving a child an allowance—a regular cash infusion—without a work connection is the same, in every respect I can see, as teaching him that money has no value. Parents who skew this lesson should be cited for child abuse on grounds they are contributing to a lifetime of misery.

Thank God, most parents take at least a decent run at the work/reward lesson. One important point, however, must be emphasized to make the lesson truly meaningful. That is, the work should not merely be done, but *done well*. This is an impressionable child drawing that weekly stipend. He *will* make a lasting connection between cash and the *way* he earns it. Anyone who ever has given a job to a young person in the real world of commerce, only to reap half-hearted and sloppy work, usually has hired someone who was equally inattentive in getting out the trash or washing dishes.

So much for the easy part.

Spending wisely is like playing the piano or gourmet cooking. It will never be quite perfect, and you must work at it all your life. It probably never will be even good unless you practice the rudiments. Most virtuosos and master chefs start very young.

The idea is not to extinguish the youthful (and adult) pleasure that comes with having a couple of nickels to rub together, but to *intensify* it. True pleasure in earning money and spending it lies in being *in total control,* in having options when opportunity or disaster come along. The difference between being in a continual boom-and-bust cycle and spending wisely is the difference between junk food and a fine meal. We are talking about an acquired taste here, and a child needs some guidance in acquiring it. So, yes, we are talking about "what's good for you," but we also are talking about *pleasure.*

All children and, sadly, many adults must learn that there is no pleasure in constantly repeating the boom-and-bust cycle. Whether every cash infusion is instantly expended by a 10-year-old at the Dairy Queen or a 25-year-old at Lord & Taylor makes little difference. The poverty side of the cycle usually will last seven times as long as the boom side, and will seem 70 times as long. You'll have a sundae in your belly or fine clothes on your frame, but in either case you'll be broke—which is never a pleasure.

Chances are that your youngster will learn about boom and bust within an hour or two of collecting his first allowance. Freshly returned from the candy store or video arcade, he will realize that he is out of options for another seven days. At that point he should be receptive to a chat about personal finance, and the pleasure of avoiding insolvency.

Realistically, when a child is very young and the cash flow is very small, you will have accomplished much if you coach him or her simply to avoid a full-blown boom-and-bust cycle. Learning that a newly arrived quarter does not have to be spent before sundown is not a bad start. (It goes without saying that your toddler should not be borrowing from the kid next door against next week's allowance.)

Eventually, age and willingness and opportunity will provide outside income in the form of lawns mowed, newspapers delivered, ice cream cones scooped, or strawberries picked at an outlying farm—whatever the local economy has to offer.

This is where the real fun begins, when a youngster's weekly cash flow exceeds a reasonable quota of trips to the candy store or arcade. "Reasonable quota" puts us in highly subjective territory, not unlike the "prevailing community standards" test of pornography. You will have your standards and I will have mine.

But at some point—possibly even when a child is still at the allowance stage—it will be critical to begin shaping a very important part of his or her adult life.

For the very first time, there will be an opportunity to teach the lesson of saving. The numbers will be small, but it is the concept, not the amount, that matters. You can talk to a youngster for hours about rainy days, but there is no substitute for his first experience of greeting a rainy day with cash reserves. Millions of modern Americans never experience the feeling in their lifetime. Similarly, there is no substitute for arriving at an especially *sunny* day—when the older kid down the block, for example, is forced to put his bike up for sale at a sweetheart price—with cash reserves.

Also for the very first time, after your offspring has demonstrated an ability to work, earn, spend wisely and save a bit, there will be an opportunity to teach the lesson of *borrowing*. Unless you decided to start reading this book in this particular paragraph, you will be (a) aware that we are dealing here with fire, and (b) possibly surprised that I am even suggesting a child buy something on credit. The first loan indeed has incendiary potential, which is exactly why it should be encountered under strong and good guidance.

Every adult who has seen a TV commercial or can add past 500 knows that a car is "the second most important investment he will ever make." (Pop quiz later on which "investment" is Number One.) Most adult victims of Living in the Future have made unrealistic choices of both house and car, among other things. Their houses and cars are too big, or too new, or were obtained with a token down payment. Many—I am tempted to say *most*—of the snazzy vehicles next to you on the expressway are something more like "the second biggest *anchor* around the driver's neck." A little guidance at a tender age, and a little experience with debt, will promote much better choices when the time comes to buy that first car.

It might be a bicycle. It might be a TV for the bedroom. Whatever it is, it represents many weeks of income and it is very important to your child. It also represents a least-pain opportunity to learn the difference between responsible use of debt and Living in the Future.

You, as the parent, must play the role of banker. You must determine and explain how your boy or girl matches up to the standards of solid credit. You must make it clear that this transaction is a matter of trust, and that how the youngster lives up to his or her end of the bargain will be a serious test of maturity—to say nothing of your patience and continuing goodwill.

You must explain the prerequisites of the deal, and delay your support if necessary until all are met.

The confidence and character tests lie with your own judgment, based on past performance in the "work hard, spend wisely and save" regimen. The youngster should know that down the road, when there are much larger deals to be made in life, the same tests will apply.

Your potential debtor must have saved enough, and have enough regular income, to make this a realistic purchase. At this youthful level we have to be subjective again, but there are some guidelines. Let's try a mythical scenario on for size.

Your son is 13 and has taken a liking to money from the first day he saw some. At an early age he left no deposit bottle at rest, either on the neighbor's lawn or in your own garage. Almost as soon as you trusted him with the power mower, he began using it around the neighborhood so often that you made him start paying for his own gas. He cheerfully and capably does his full share around the house, so you never got around to cutting off his allowance even though he now has outside income. His allowance disappears every week in one trip to watch Arnold Schwarzenegger or Chuck Norris at the local eight-screen. He dips into his own earnings occasionally to finance an even more luxurious social life or a bizarre piece of apparel that you refuse to buy for him. Nonetheless, he has managed to reach June 1 with $86 stashed someplace that neither you nor he can identify, but where his mother can retrieve it on demand.

Clearly this young man is in the running on grounds of character and confidence. The cash test will depend on income, and on what he seeks to finance.

Current income stands at $35 a week—$10 allowance and a steady $25 from mowing lawns. What he wants to buy, for $150, is a year-old bike that sold for $350 new. He's talking about using it for a paper route, but none is available at the moment, so the bike must be viewed as a pleasure purchase. What he wants to do is spend 80 of his dollars and borrow 70 of yours.

An awful lot seems more than reasonable here, but sit down and go over a couple of facts with him.

First of all, he has done a first-class job of maintaining a rainy-day fund. But it's really not wise to wipe out 90 percent of your savings to make a down payment on *anything,* even with that kind of equity.

Second of all, and despite the incredibly long payment schedules that lenders entice us with, it is never a good idea to reach any further into the future than absolutely necessary. Let's see, at age 13, for a bicycle, how about 10 weekly payments? That'll leave three weeks before school starts, time enough to load up for the next big round of spending.

So let's say he uses $50—closer to half of his savings—as a

down payment on this major purchase. That means you will be lending him $100, and his payments will be $10 a week. (The *week* part of it is important; give him as many chances as possible to be reminded of debt's down side.) As part of the deal, he will continue to *save* $5 a week. (Saving is not a discretionary part of budgeting, or it won't happen.) He will still maintain $20 a week discretionary income for the duration of the loan. At the end of the loan term, he will have $4 more in savings than when he started. Meanwhile, if the paper route happens to come through, it'll be found money for him.

That makes a neat little paradigm, one that I think is reasonable even though you will have talked your son into borrowing *more* than he asked for. That, you will recall, was to preserve savings. If the resultant payments had come to more than $10 a week, I probably would have told the boy to find a cheaper bike or wait until he had saved some more.

The only problem I see is that your son's weekly payments are exactly equal to his weekly allowance. I think I'd make the payments fall due on a different day of the week, just to make sure he sees the money change hands.

Your son should also know that he will be sleeping in the garage with his bike if he decides to make another major purchase before this one is paid off.

And, oh yes, pray that your town doesn't go six weeks without rain for those lawns.

It seems so simple. But how many adults can say their personal finances are so well-reasoned and under control? Probably many of those who can't did not get a chance to make those $10 payments on a bicycle, while Mom and Dad made sure the game plan was followed every step of the way.

14

The Terror of the Teens

It would be handy if we could outline the evolution of our financial personalities as a seamless passage from cradle to credit card. Teenagers, however, need a chapter all their own.

Teens tend to view yesterday as irrelevant and tomorrow as a place farther away than Afghanistan. Teens also tend to believe that tomorrow, if and when it ever arrives, will be very, very big for them. This mind-set clearly will cause difficulty in relating to numerous realities. Money is right at the head of the list.

Since this is a first-person book, and since I fervently hope that a few teenagers are reading it, I have to say up front that I did some incredibly dumb things in my teens. I thought I was indestructible and immortal. I paid ridiculous attention to what my peers thought and wore and did. I made a good income but, despite having no obligation to support anyone but myself, blew it as fast as it came in—eventually *faster* than it came in. I *knew* that my future would be big, and therefore was concerned only for my present. I am embarrassed at the way I behaved, in many arenas. In other words, I was a typical teenager.

What a weird time of life. Older people usually have two things in common. First, they'd like to be young again. Second, they wouldn't be teenagers for all the designer jeans in California. Give us a glance again at 25, maybe, or even 30-something. Or let us go one more time on that wonderful fishing trip when we were 10. But please, please, no more pimples and peer pressure. No more clinging to childhood and panting for adulthood. How did I ever survive? Once is enough!

Financially, many people never do recover from those wild and crazy years. So, as much as we'd like to, we can't erase the teen years from any discussion of personal finances. That would be approximately the same as erasing the Civil War from a discussion of how the United States got from 1776 to 1992.

It seems that every aspect of financial health, just as in physical health, cries out for early intervention. That's why Rule One for surviving the teens in financially fit condition can be found in the previous chapter—pre-teen education. Rule Two does not exist in any codified form.

The dynamics of teenagehood resemble the dynamics of hurricane season in southern Florida. As the parent of a teenager, you know a big wind will come one day. You watch the early warning signals. You prepare for it. When it hits, you batten down the hatches and improvise as necessary. When the storm passes, you hope that nature and your preventive measures have held damage to a minimum. If not, you must start over from scratch.

Why so?

More than anything, I believe, the curse of the teen years derives from the need to fit in, to be accepted, to feel a part of the crowd. That's a normal human inclination. But in the teens the phenomenon reaches near-pathological dimensions. In its extreme, such as street gangs, it *is* pathological.

In no way do I wish to make light of the teenagers' psychological dilemma. If life is an unending series of transitions, none is as difficult as this one. No wonder that the herd instinct is at its strongest in the teen years, or that suicide regularly and tragically occurs among people who have barely begun to live.

Nature brings young men and women (old boys and girls) to their physical peak before they compile a stitch of real-life experience. While they are still "going out to play," it is their bodies that the Pentagon summons to crawl through jungles and get shot at.

In modern times, technology has seemed to be aimed squarely at adolescent hormones and culture. The automobile took young couples out of the family drawing room and into the back seat. The Pill took nature's consequence out of sex. The electric guitar created a new, raucous music. The transistor made every corner of the universe a party place. The drug labs produced chemicals that made a Saturday night six-pack look like spring water. The cathode ray tube pumped graphic images, and the illusion of experience, into young minds—forever changing the way future generations will *think*.

TV above all is a marketing device that loves the herd instinct in general, and young minds in particular. Keeping Up with Johnny is a targetable phenomenon among pre-teens. In the teenaged years, it is a gold mine for advertisers. Teens have more money and more options for buying an answer to that overwhelming need of acceptance by their peers.

What is the bottom line for the teenager—and for parents who desperately try to keep in touch with their sons and daughters, often by footing the bills? The cost of Keeping Up with Johnny is astronomical. As a child of the '50s and a parent of teenagers, I can assure you that—although the herd instinct has not changed—the price tag has been enlarged by several zeroes.

Designer clothing certainly has come a long way. If you would have told me, or my parents, that sophistication, sex appeal, marquee names, inflated prices and every twist of the "must-have" mentality would envelop the *blue jean* industry, we would have called EMS on your behalf.

Or how about athletics? Except for a couple of truly gifted jocks in every high school, sports was something we did for entertainment and exercise and to play out macho competitive instincts. Most kids in the '50s owned a baseball glove and a pair of "gym shoes," period. Today, the parents of a 12-year-old playing hockey spend more inflation-adjusted dollars to prepare for a single season than my parents spent on sports equipment from kindergarten through high school. In some cases, a single pair of today's running shoes will make a car payment.

Vacations? I thought that was the summertime, a space between grades when you went out, had a good time and made some money. I admit I blew the money, but that's not the point.

Cars? It was a lot easier to be a part of the crowd in the '50s, because so few high school students had wheels. Today, teenaged car pools are commonplace because the school parking lots are full. In well-heeled suburbs in northern states, some kids have two cars—one for summer, one for winter.

Spending money? If today's high-schooler is fortunate enough to have a work ethic, but also possesses an unfortunate compulsion to attend every hot rock concert and every important ballgame, he would have to spread sauce on a few thousand Big Macs a week just to keep himself in tickets.

No matter how many billion burgers have been sold, that's not what's happening. Instead, parental subsidies are growing larger and lasting longer. We see very little of the teenager who divides 95 percent of his time between work and school. The emphasis falls squarely on the two E's: education and entertainment. And I am not aware of any strong trend among parents to re-emphasize the W word.

Some of this, I am sure, results from parents' empathy with the very real and very scary obstacles that modern kids must negotiate. No amount of nostalgia for the '50s, or any other version of a simpler life, can erase the realities of crack cocaine and AIDS and the rest of the menu of horrors teens must face today. On the other hand, you are doing your offspring a great disservice if you award the Exemplary Teenaged Achievement Medal for no greater accomplishment than remaining drug-free. There is more to life than just saying no.

I have said that most teenagers do dumb things, and that inevitably there comes a time when talking long-term sense to your adolescent son or daughter will be like talking to air. That always has been, and always will be, true. There is a difference, however, between a parent accepting that fact and a parent becoming a co-conspirator in dumb strategies.

The stereotypical parent/teen pattern in late 20th-Century middle-class America is one that in my opinion is guaranteed to diminish self-esteem in the youngster. It also drags two generations at once into Living in the Future. In other words, the family that borrows together, sorrows together.

What happens is that the teenager yearns mightily for independence but finds that keeping up with his peers—who always, somehow, have enough money to maintain the lifestyle *du jour*—is impossible. The parents are eternally grateful that their child has not turned to coke-snorting, and are desperate to maintain communication with a loved one who appears to be drifting into a new sphere of influence. Keeping Up with the Joneses becomes a sort of cross-generational shared experience. After all, you don't want your kid to be the only one who isn't dressed in the proper uniform, or the only one not making the spring trip to Florida.

The teenager becomes more and more reliant on his parents, the very ones from which he is aching to assert some independence. He loses self-esteem in the process. It is little surprise if he becomes more defiant than grateful.

The parents, getting nowhere when they confront issues, nonetheless begin to mortgage their own future to maintain peace and stability in the home.

What a recipe!

An explosion might be a relief. More likely, the pain is like a toothache—constant, nagging, beneath the surface.

The situation varies significantly in degree, onset and duration from home to home. In some homes, of course, it doesn't occur at all. In some homes it is not a nagging toothache but an open, festering wound.

You can see why there is no tidy Rule Two for teenaged lessons of Living in the Future. You can be reasonably tidy with guidelines for younger kids, for young adults, for newlyweds, for mid-life couples, even for multimillion-dollar corporations. Teenagers, in their own way, are far more volatile and complex than any of the above. Teens are neither fish nor fowl—part child, part adult. Circumstances of their day-to-day lives require financial compromise and creativity.

A few teens are workaholics. A few are even anti-materialist. But whatever a teen is at the moment, he may be something entirely different a week or two from now. A kid who never cracked a book can become a scholar late in the game. An honor roll student can decide that school is nice, but he would rather go straight into the work place than into college. Either might test the waters, then change his mind.

Amid all this turmoil, the fact is that very few teens today can achieve total financial independence. This is a radical change in our lives, too radical to be dismissed as a change in lifestyle. It is almost a biological change, a lengthening of the gestation period that leads to adulthood.

I was supporting myself somewhat before I left high school, and went straight from graduation to full-fledged membership in the adult financial community. This was no achievement. It was commonplace in the '50s.

Now, the days of picking up summer jobs at factory wages are over. Often, a car is necessary to maintain even a part-time job that barely maintains the car. Half the educational or career paths available require a personal computer in the bedroom at an early age. More than half require schooling beyond high school, which means even more prolonged reliance on Mom and Dad. At today's cost of schooling and today's prevailing wages, a part-time job will barely supply spending money—let alone tuition, room, board and transportation. Even if a teenager is fighting against Keeping Up with the Joneses, living is not cheap.

At the end of this tortured path, we all hope and pray, will emerge a productive person who has a marketable skill and who is in touch with financial reality. What in the world will help assure that outcome?

Rule One, pre-teen education, offers a foundation.

Rule Two, if I could somehow crystalize a useful bromide, would rely heavily on the W word. It is of utmost importance that work become an important part of a teenager's life, far more important than whether or not the wages received make ends meet.

On a personal level, this is about self-esteem, and the nurturing of discipline that will contribute to happiness for a very long life to come. Tomorrow, contrary to standard teenaged opinion, *will* arrive—and again and again and again.

On a broader level, the connection between reward and work well done is perhaps, after procreation, what makes the world go around. Too many of our young people have lost that connection. Ask any employer.

If a teen is going to lead the subsidized life, it should be assumed that education, not entertainment, will be the bigger of the two E's. And it should be assumed that work will consume the majority of time not consumed by education. That is an 18-year-old's option, of course, having reached the age of majority in all matters except alcohol. But it is not an option that he should be able to choose on his parents' money.

Even though a teenager's income isn't covering costs, it should be managed as if it were. Otherwise, the teen years become a short (or long) course in how to destroy all that sound financial conditioning that was supposed to be built up in childhood. This means that a teen should:

- Prepare and follow a budget. Parents should know the exact due dates and amounts of any major expenses, such as sports fees or class trips or tuition, in which they have agreed to participate. Teens should avoid the inexplicable embarrassment of constant insolvency at 17 after having been able, at 12, to make a cash infusion last a week.
- Save some money. Five measly bucks a week? Why not? It's the habit, not the amount, that's important. Sound accounting principles will reveal that this is actually increasing the weekly parental subsidy by $5. But it might be the best-spent $5 of all. Have a parent/teen agreement on the way this fund can be used.
- Live in the present. Anyone living on a subsidy has no business charging purchases. Parents who skirt the entire

budgeting process by handing over a credit card probably did not let their kids play with guns when they were younger, but the effect is similar.

* * *

As I said, this is a time for improvisation and creativity. You will, I hope, find your own best ways to help your teenager, in his or her special circumstances, stay in touch with financial reality.

Think of all the effort, on the part of both teen and parent, as an investment in the future. It's not a question of saving a buck today, but of saving grief down the road.

This much I know: I went through a decade of financial torture as a young adult. That's because I came out of my teen-aged years insolvent, with lousy spending habits, with no savings, but with plenty of bills. The ensuing torture was a natural progression.

One of my sons, having finally passed through the terrible teens, gave me a coffee mug that I keep on my desk. The message on it—which you may have seen in the gift shops—illustrates the new perspective that most of us acquire once the teens are behind us. The mug says:

"Dear Dad,

"In answer to the questions you've asked me over the years:

"1. Yes, I thought you owned the electric company.

"2. I don't know what the hell I thought I was doing.

"3. Yes, I actually did think you were made of money."

15

Hitting the Books

Many associates in my firm possess fine college degrees. I am sure they are quite tired of hearing one particular battle-worn McTevia-ism around our conference table. It's something I probably spout too often, usually when the solution to a problem at hand can be found only in experience and not in a lecture or a textbook, even of the MBA type. (Which is to say, practically all the time.) The line I seem to have trouble suppressing is this: "I don't have a piece of paper on the wall to prove I'm smart."

Financially successful people without a degree are an endangered species. We are a very large group, but our average age must be ancient. Sometimes it seems that most people under 40 who can walk and chew gum simultaneously can also name a college in their resume. The glut of degrees has led many employers to demand a sheepskin in job classifications where the connection is flimsy at best. Weeding out the illiterate and mathematically ignorant is always a good idea. But given the cost of college today, it would seem that more cost-effective means are available. And that says nothing of the injustice befalling bright, confident, capable applicants who flunk the litmus test.

We have nearly become a society that assumes four or more years of education beyond high school. Many young people are allowed to slide along that time line, reaching deep into their

20s and into their parents' pocketbooks, without the least idea of where they are bound. To my mind, that is not education; that is hanging out with the meter running. The fact is, even in today's education-oriented world, important choices must be made by both parents and students. The most basic choices involve assessing what a particular education will be worth, how much it will cost, how it will be paid for, and who will pay for it. Because in today's world, an automobile quite likely will *not* be the second biggest investment of a person's lifetime. The price of that diploma has reached Mercedes and Rolls-Royce territory, and very few graduates will be driving those particular nameplates.

In terms of personal finance, a college education can be a most valuable tool—or it can be useless, depending on the type of degree and how well it is earned. A degree of any kind can be *worse* than useless if a mother and father live too far into the future in order to provide an education for their child, or if the student learns not much except to rely entirely on others to survive the lean years.

Furthermore, if a student emerges from college with a skewed concept of the lifelong financial marathon that is about to begin, then he or she shortly will be very young, very well-educated, and very bankrupt. It happens all the time. The people who are best-educated and have the best jobs seem to be the people most burdened by debt. Every week I see clients who are smart, educated and sinking into the worst financial jackpots imaginable. I look at them and say, "How could you ever have thought that you could carry this off?" My conclusion has to be that an education has only made them more creative in their efforts to undertake debt.

Even in a good economy, some products of the degree glut would be "underemployed." In a soft economy, one can find MA's bussing tables and Ph.D's driving cabs. A college degree, generically speaking and in regard to income, doesn't guarantee a thing and often doesn't count for much. Even among the best and brightest, no good future lies in training for a job that doesn't exist.

Notice the phrase "training for a job." A good deal of the millions of man hours and dollars devoted to our higher education system have nothing to do with career preparation, or with making a student a productive member of society. That is OK, I guess, although I shudder at the idea of my tax dollars supporting legions of obscure inquiries into the motivation of characters in obscure plays, or into the lifestyle of of the lower class in 12th-Century Holland. Much of what transpires in academia strikes me as a more costly and less amusing version of the old Bill Cosby routine, "Why is there air?" If you're breathing, you should know the answer. If you're not, it doesn't matter a great deal.

I leave that one for the philosophers. And I hope they have a private grant for their work.

You cannot discuss personal finance without discussing education, however. And that means discussing the relationship between income and schooling, something that is too often ignored, obscured or misjudged.

For starters, let's recognize that not everyone will go to college. And that not all of those who bypass college are drug addicts or losers of some other type. Perhaps they cannot afford college. Perhaps they have obligations to earn a living immediately. Perhaps their verbal skills are not above the median. Perhaps they already are embarked on a career that does not require college. Whatever the reason, the Constitution neither guarantees a college degree nor requires one for citizenship, productivity and self-esteem.

At the low end, some non-college jobs are indispensable but menial. As work stoppages prove from time to time, an absence of garbage pickup can make life difficult in the most educated neighborhoods. Indispensable as such jobs may be, they are not a solid reason for choosing against college.

Many non-college jobs, however, are neither menial nor dispensable nor without financial reward. If there were no mechanics, no tool and die craftsmen, no photocopy repairmen, no salespersons—or a thousand other job classifications—the economy would grind to a halt. A good many of these workers earn an income surpassing that of a good many college graduates. These jobs most often require some verbal skills and/or some math. They might require some trade school. The college graduates one increasingly finds working these jobs may not be underemployed so much as over-degreed or mis-degreed. Very likely they are among that group who slide from high school into college without much thought of why they are enrolling and where they are headed. Perhaps they attended too many seminars on "Why is there air?," or they have a degree in modern American cinema.

Which leads us back to basic, simple choices. Whether you are a great thinker or just another entry in life's marathon, an advanced education is one of the most expensive things you ever will purchase. If you never buy a house, an education likely will be your *most expensive* purchase. Obviously, such an investment should be assessed carefully. You must place a value on it—both actuarially (in terms of how much income it is likely to produce) and subjectively (what it is worth to you in non-productive terms, especially if you are going to study modern American cinema). You must assess your ability to pay. And you must assess your willingness to delay gratification—either by going to school part-time while earning a living, or by living frugally after graduation while you pay the bill.

There is nothing wrong, by the way, with figuratively signing a mortgage to pay for an education. If a college degree is that important to you, it simply becomes one of your life's major purchases. That will work, as long as you understand exactly what it is that you are doing. If, on the other hand, you are one of those lost souls who regard a college degree as a birthright like air and water, then you are in serious trouble.

As with any major purchase, either the money must be saved in advance, or gratification must be delayed somewhere along the line. You cannot come charging out of college, mortgaged degree in hand, and reach for the new car and the condo and the vacation and all the rest of the grown-up toys. You cannot assume that tomorrow will take care of today. Part of your unknown tomorrow already has been spent on that diploma. It's time to sweat a little, not to party. Keep that scenario firmly in mind when you sign the mortgage.

That's the financing side of the educational purchase. The more fundamental side—what *kind* of education are you going to buy?—remains a source of great perplexity to me. High school students, their parents and educational institutions consistently fail to make the connection between a particular course of study and a productive place in society.

Our grade schools and high schools, for example, should not only be helping to educate our young people in personal economics —how to stay out of financial trouble—but should also be channeling students into areas of the work place where they will be able to earn a living. I can't see why the educational system, or parents, deserve passing grades on either count.

It takes more than saying, "What do you want to be when you grow up?" A youngster might want to be the next Toscannini or the next Picasso—or for that matter, the next grade-school music teacher or art teacher. All are admirable goals; but what if no jobs will be available, not with the New York Philharmonic and not with the local grade school?

The law of supply and demand has been bent cockeyed for decades in this regard. Our higher educational institutions, and their feeder schools, answer the demand of dreamy-eyed students rather than the demand of the real-world marketplace. Scores of students will pour forth from journalism schools for every decent-paying newspaper job that opens up in the next decade, many of which will be taken by seasoned reporters and editors laid off elsewhere. Meanwhile, our graduate engineering schools are dominated by *foreign* students, who apparently possess much more solid awareness of the connection between education and making a productive living.

What I am suggesting is not, of course, that engineering is somehow more noble than journalism. The point is, as much effort should be directed to charting employers' needs in various degree fields as is directed to asking why there is air. Then, young people coming up through the grade schools and high schools should be given, along with their parents, a solid under-standing of what the data reveal. Investing untold millions of dollars in career-specific degrees for which there are no careers strikes me as the educational establishment's own appropriately nebulous version of Living in the Future.

If a young person insists on a calling in which few are chosen, so be it—so long as he is prepared to put his degree in a desk drawer and do something else for a living. Parents might well think twice about participating in such an investment.

Opening up the parental pocketbook to finance advanced education is, in any case, a most serious step in the financial marathon for all three parties—mother, father and student.

The first consideration should be the fact that nothing in the law or common sense or moral codes requires a parent to pay for a son's or daughter's college degree. Worst of all, parents should not bankrupt themselves to do so, any more than they would bankrupt themselves and jeopardize their marriage to buy a car or a house for an offspring.

If you are among those who believe it *is* your obligation to provide an advanced education for your children, then the obli-gation begins the day a child is born—not the day the enroll-ment fee is due. Buy a life insurance policy or an annuity or some other instrument in the infant's name and send him off with your blessing 18 years later, without disrupting your life. It's the only sensible way.

My own belief is that if a young person wants an education badly enough, and knows in advance that it will not be his just for the asking, he will find a way to obtain it. He will strive for a scholarship, work and save, and—if necessary—delay enroll-ment or study part-time while in the work place. If a student contributes substantially toward the cost of school, a parent who is not interested in footing the bill might well pitch in and help—just as you would with a child in any tight but honest situation. Those students who must fully or substantially fi-nance their own educations, by the way, tend not to make frivo-lous choices or waste a class.

I gained some recent experience in the validity of treating education as part of the whole life financial experience rather than as a birthright that fills the time from age 18 to age 22.

Joan had become friends with a young woman who lives near our house in Florida. The neighbor, frustrated because at 31 she was wrestling with financial problems while trying to complete her education, asked Joan if we would consider helping her. Joan suggested that the three of us talk.

It became apparent that not only did she seek help with her education, but with living expenses as well. Her frustration was rooted in the fact that she was working part-time, going to school part-time, and would need two to three years to get her degree. The less painful route appeared to lie in finding an angel who would lend her money to finance full-time tuition, as well as the living expenses she wouldn't be able to handle while carrying a full load of classes.

It also became apparent that she was hopelessly insolvent, and that repaying such a loan would require her, upon graduation, to work five years at an as-yet non-existent job—at a salary she agreed would be difficult to find without any experience.

The next day, after she had gathered information I requested, we sat down and in two hours developed a plan that closely follows the McTevia Model for debt restructuring.

Without going further into debt to an angel or anyone else, but with an investment of her own discipline, we constructed a plan that would rid her of the sleepless nights she had been experiencing for several years. She was overwhelmed at the unforeseen benefits of such a radically simple approach.

She would whittle at her debt by following my well-developed plan while working part-time in a job related to her field of study. At graduation time, she was excited to learn, not only would she have a diploma and three years' related experience, but she would be debt-free and absolutely on her own. This fiercely independent woman had tears in her eyes as she saw the true independence that would accompany her degree.

Days later, we learned that she was eating properly again,

sleeping well, and had acquired an entirely different outlook on life.

The anecdote mixes apples (education) and oranges (strategies for attacking financial crises). They should be mixed more often.

16

The Material World

We cannot leave personal finance without taking a critical look at our relationship with *things*.

Toys. Perks. Baubles. Goodies.

Material goods.

A pyramid of influences has enticed modern Americans into Living in the Future: bad habits nurtured since childhood; lack of financial education; peer pressure and herd instinct; media exhortations; easy credit. No one could quarrel with that list. It's as safe as talking about the weather. But when you come to the keystone of the Great Pyramid, materialism, a certain apprehension invades the dialogue. Are we drifting from finance into metaphysics, from accounting into religion?

Not really. The most dispassionate, empirical, numbers-crunching analysis of Living in the Future must address our distorted value system. To do otherwise would be to photograph an elephant through a microscope.

Something very basic has to be at work here, something bigger than the number of plastic cards in our wallets. Covetousness antedates revolving charge accounts by several thousand years, but I think it is safe to say that consummated lust for consumer goods has reached an unparalleled plateau in modern America. Some commentators lamented that, with the collapse of the Soviet Union, the former communist subjects would be importing our materialism but not our ideals. Sometimes I wonder if materialism has not, in fact, become our dominant ideal. Certainly if the former Soviets begin to measure their lives in technogadgets and designer jeans, as other distant populations already have, it is not because *they* invented the standard. What they see is what they see get.

It is impossible to delve as deeply into personal and corporate finance as I have, for as long as I have, and come away without being awestruck at the intensity to which relationships between people and things can grow. The most hopeless financial mazes become ever more grotesque and the tallest tar paper towers soar ever higher because their architects desperately do not want to cast adrift even a bit of the store-bought imagery that has come to define their being.

Am I suggesting that making a good income and being willing to spend much of it on things that make life comfortable and pleasurable is wrong? Of course not. That is, in fact, a fair description of my own lifestyle.

Am I suggesting that many Americans, however, become so addicted to *consuming* that their relationships with people become secondary to their relationships with things? So addicted to material rewards that they can't think straight? So addicted that they, and their finances, career out of control? Absolutely.

And that is why it is necessary, at the risk of treading into territory of philosophy and belief, to stop for a moment and recognize materialism as a distinct piece of the personal finance puzzle.

At some point we must consider—not only as a matter of our personal value systems, but as a simple, pragmatic part of running life's marathon—just how much wealth we want to squander on image. So much materialistic spending does not acquire anything "material" at all. Instead it "makes a statement," as they say. The fact is, a luxury car will not get you to work one minute faster than a subcompact, and Geraldo will still be Geraldo on a $5,000 ultrascreen TV.

Yes, the bigger car and the bigger TV are better. As a

responsible consumer you must ask whether the bigger car is $20,000 better, whether the bigger TV is $4,500 better. More importantly, you must ask whether that is the real reason you are acquiring it. And more important yet, are you buying it with real money or with future income—which, of course, does not yet exist, and may never exist?

An addicted materialist living in the present is one thing. If we flog him too hard, we are indeed crossing the boundary into religion or its close cousin. Seldom, however, does one find a hard-core materialist living in the present, unless he is extremely wealthy. And a hard-core materialist Living in the Future invariably is a case for financial EMS.

The substance-abuse counselors speak of a doubly desperate phenomenon: "co-dependency." Liquor and drugs, for example, make for a lethal whole that is greater than the sum of its parts. So it goes with acute materialism. If you are addicted to material things, if you make them more important than they really are, if you define your life on a materialistic scoreboard—then you will spend every last mortgageable piece of your future. You will be co-dependent on toys and credit, lifestyle and leverage.

Without backing off for one moment from the proposition that there is nothing wrong with driving a solid and stylish automobile, or wearing a superior suit of clothes, or sipping a glass of fine wine, I suggest that none of these things is worth having if the future must be mortgaged to get it. In that case we are indulging not only in materialism, but in *phony* materialism, playing role games with mortgaged toys. Even the drug pushers then become one up on us. They may define their lives in terms of wheels and threads, but at least the pusher always pays in cash.

Phony materialism represents the worst of all the financial ills that I believe begin in childhood, which is where they most likely are correctable. The key, after all, is *the need to have it at all costs*. Tell me how a consumer who adds an expensive impulse—a Rolex, say, or a high-fashion dress—to an already burdened debt service is really any different than a 12-year-old who will *die* unless he has the newest Nintendo game? At least the 12-year-old has parents who might teach him something about money and try to influence his value system. No one will intervene with the adult in the department store except marriage counselors and bankruptcy attorneys, both of whom might be needed in due course.

Every abusive addiction extracts its price from the user. The materialistic credit junkie pays with his freedom. For all his toys, the materialistic credit junkie totally has forsaken his independence. When a vast majority of your paycheck goes to debt service, you are not free. There are people in our society, not entrepreneurs but well-paid employees making over $100,000 a year, who live to the full extent of their debt service. They are counting on their employer to pay them even more money next year, or the year after. What they will do then, of course, is acquire a larger debt service. Their financial sophistication goes not one step beyond a child counting on a larger allowance with his next birthday.

Ask these people if they would prefer to stop the merry-go-round, to get off and spend more time with their families, or go fishing or camping, and many will say: "God, yes. But I'm trapped. I just started a 30-year mortgage. I've got bills you wouldn't believe."

Of course they do. And why? Is it because you can't make it today on $150,000 a year? Hardly. It's because materialistic values have pushed their debt service sky-high. Remember the young man who told me a family of four couldn't make it on $750 a week? Plug in any number within reason. It doesn't matter at all. $750. $1,000. $1,500. And up. You will hear the same mournful cry. Burdened by the debt of phony materialism, people lose their freedom and assert, in all seriousness, that they "cannot make it on $1,500 a week."

Remember our mythical young Bill Dunn? His case was intentionally simplistic, so as to make debt analysis and restructuring readily understandable. But even in his case, stated in balance-sheet terms, we left young Bill shedding not just a car payment, but some of his materialistic values as well. The change was enforced by necessity, but in that sad circumstance often comes revelation. Bill Dunn—and millions of Americans—have placed unrealistic value on *things,* have acquired them with unrealistic debt, and have paid for them with their freedom. That's why Bill was so upbeat in his reduced state: He saw himself becoming free, having options, being in control.

Young Bill is getting his marathon equation balanced with just $26,000 on the income side. If he is like most young people, he probably believes, deep down, that there is nothing wrong with materialistic values that couldn't be solved by a large boost to his income. Well, the arithmetic works. Reality is something else.

In my practice, I advise people whose personal finances, or whose golden goose company—or both—are headed straight for the tank. Sometimes such people blithely continue to "buy" the most luxurious toys and the most trendy ski trips with no currency but a personal signature. For them, life simply does not exist without the toys of affluence. Their image statement no longer holds even a grain of truth, but it is boldly asserted anyway, as long as the words can be found to say it.

In other cases, there is nothing the least blithe about a lofty victim's behavior in the face of financial disaster. The dynamic is the same: defining self-worth in terms of material well-being. But the result is tragedy.

Five times in my career, clients found the pain of discarding material goods literally too intense to bear. Rather than restructuring their lives, they took their lives. Rather than recognizing that they had a financial problem, meeting it head on, going home and talking to their wives and children, shedding the fine address and the fine cars and moving on, they killed themselves. Five times! How incredibly tragic.

All five were business owners living far above the average lifestyle. They were people commonly described as millionaires, though at the end they may simply have been living like millionaires. One was a newcomer to high affluence. Four were born into families that had been living at that level for years. It is a whole different thing when affluence has been sustained into the third, fourth and fifth generations. The embarrassment and humiliation of financial crisis are magnified to a degree that the Bill Dunns of the world can barely contemplate. It is a lesson worth reflecting upon.

There is pain and agony in a financial crisis no matter your level of affluence. My own experience, however, clearly shows that a victim who possesses firsthand knowledge that life can exist without toys and image statements will fare by far the best. A first-generation entrepreneur, someone who once worked at the grunt level, usually can go back to the lifestyle he knew 10 or 20 years earlier. Often, in fact, he believes he can rise up again. When the handwriting is on the wall, he will say: "Well, I've done this before; let's start over." I have seen some learn by their mistakes and emerge more successful than ever.

It is audacious, I know, for a man who leads a very good life by materialist standards to mount a soapbox and exhort you to stop and smell the roses, to enjoy the sunrises that nature brings you free of charge, to define yourself least of all by the goods that you acquire. I think you now can see that this is not street-corner preaching, but sound professional advice. I heartily believe it to be good for the soul. I *know* it to be good for your financial health.

Strictly speaking I am, as they said when I began to build my practice by word of mouth, "a numbers man." The message I so dearly wish to convey here is that if you keep score with nothing but numbers, then you will be a sure loser.

PART THREE

Companies in Trouble

17

Only the Zeroes Are Different

I think it is easy for anyone to understand the individual financial marathon, to fathom how our mythical young Bill Dunn
outpaced his $26,000 income, to comprehend how a person in
financial trouble solves his problem by withdrawing from the
future and living in the present. Now I'd like to convince you
that when the checking account and the due bills are corporate
or institutional, nothing really changes but the size of the problem.

The dollars on the bottom line increase by huge numbers,
as do the number of people experiencing pain and agony. When
a Bill Dunn reorganizes, no one notices except his parents and
a few creditors with relatively puny sums at risk. When a corporation with hundreds or thousands of employees and millions of
dollars of debt reorganizes, *everybody* notices. Of course, if a few
hundred thousand Bill Dunns must reorganize all at once, their
aggregate misery and financial impact exceed that of any corporation—but that's one for the economists and historians to sort
out.

Here, I'd like to share my inside vantage point to illustrate
that it is a simple and direct path from wooing childhood goddesses with leveraged movie tickets to presiding over the decline
and fall of a substantial, once-prosperous company. And to show

that, just as Bill Dunn took appropriate action by withdrawing into the present, corporate managers who stay flexible enough to keep operations in line with current realities are a giant step ahead of the game.

Simplistic analyses always draw heat, and I expect my full share. I like to think, however, that someone who has led the reorganization of as many as 50 companies per year can offer valid observations on the process. And for the life of me, I cannot view the financial core of these troubled situations—and the basis of their solution—as anything but *simple*.

Notice I did not say "easy." There is a difference. Flight is a simple concept, but my grandfather and the Wright brothers were contemporaries. It wasn't easy for man to get into the air, and the average person floating above the clouds in a jetliner today can't explain how he got there. Einstein's theory of relativity consists of three letters and two symbols. What could be simpler—and less easy—than that?

I don't mean to suggest, of course, that matters of budgeting and credit and financial integrity are somehow on an intellectual plane with aerodynamics or advanced physics. I merely mean to note that sometimes the simple facts of how things work broach difficulties of understanding, reveal hard realities and defy popular embrace.

The simple fact is that Bill Dunn discovered he would be in perpetual crisis unless he increased his income or decreased expenses or did both. When General Motors Chairman Robert Stempel went before the TV cameras in late 1991 and announced that the flagship of American industry was about to downsize, something considerably larger than Bill Dunn's $2,600-a-month reality was at stake. The principle, however, is identical. Algae and whales live in the same sea.

So there was absolutely nothing "shocking" in the "news" from GM, though some of the less-skilled commentators chose to describe it that way. When the financial equation doesn't balance, you must adjust it—if you can. GM's equation had become painfully and obviously out of balance, and it was just a question of when an adjustment would be made. If you worked for GM, of course, you also had a strong desire to know *where.*

I was driving down I-94 outside Detroit when I heard the GM press conference on my car radio. There is nothing whatsoever amusing about the troubles of an industrial giant, particularly when its world headquarters sit smack in the middle of the region where you do much of your business. Nonetheless, I had to chuckle as I listened to the frenzied news coverage, because Robert Stempel—pumping the bilges of a listing supership—was about to negotiate the very same shoals navigated by skippers of lesser vessels, from dinghy to freighter. In troubled financial waters, every crewman and every passenger has his own agenda and his own priorities. Stempel would be hearing—loudly, plaintively, angrily—from every one of them. I have played through this scenario so very many times. Now here was the granddaddy of all modern companies following the same script, adapted for a wide-screen Cecil B. DeMille production with a cast of thousands.

In the case of GM, with plants and employees spread across the nation and in some cases providing the lifeblood of entire communities, "decreasing expenses" means pulling the plug on thousands of good people who have done nothing to deserve their fate. Governors, senators, mayors and union leaders get on the phone, get organized and get into the news. Assembly workers with wives and children and mortgages are not much interested in the fact that their livelihood represents cargo that must be tossed overboard to save the ship. A sad analogy, but a true one. The financial equation is simple and immutable, whether it is unbalanced by a middle-class couple's new station wagon—or by a huge corporation's surplus factories. All the separate agendas and all the personal tragedies generated by corporate belt-tightening, compelling as they may be, obscure the financial simplicity of it all.

In my own practice, I do not reorganize the General Motorses of the world. However, I have restructured several companies and institutions doing more than $200 million in annual business. I have done the same for scores of organizations in the $25-$100 million range. And I would have to do a serious archives search to count the number of retail stores and small manufacturing plants I have restructured or, unfortunately, guided through liquidation. In *every* case, a relatively simple proposition acquires a complicated texture because of the separate agendas brought to the table. Each of those agendas represents, by extension, a piece of the future that my client has been living in.

Let's take, as an example, a restructuring case that has found its way to bankruptcy court under Chapter XI. Court is not the best place to be for this process, as you will see later in more detail. But for now, let's say that the Ajax Company—fighting the good fight to reorganize and save itself from extinction—wishes to shut down an assembly plant to help bring its financial equation into balance. The bankruptcy judge will find assembled before him a sizable number of people, each billing a sizable fee to the dwindling Ajax bank account, and each with his own selfish agenda:

- James V. McTevia, whose agenda is to help his client restructure Ajax and save it.
- An attorney also representing my debtor client, because—even though I am the one formulating the plan—I am not an attorney and therefore cannot lead the argument of its merits in court.
- An attorney representing the bank whose line of credit to Ajax is at risk.
- An attorney representing the employees of the jeopardized plant, for whom no good can come of the shutdown—but which, believe me, must happen if Ajax is to survive.
- An attorney representing Ajax's industrial creditors, many of whom wish to sell the company's assets—right down to the last paper clip—this afternoon.

Also on hand may well be one or more representatives of various taxing authorities, who in some cases will have precedence over all of the above interests in extracting a share of Ajax's carcass.

You begin to see how a simple matter of bringing expenses and income into balance becomes muddied and made to seem much more complex than it really is. By overmortgaging its future, Ajax has attracted a swarm of wolves to its door, each howling for a chunk of Ajax's present. And now, to a simple equation, lawyers will bring points of law, accountants will bring crunches and spins, union leaders will bring cries for social justice, the taxman will bring as close a thing as we can find to certitude in this life, and, hopefully, the judge will bring infinite wisdom. With six people in one room billing as much as $300 an hour for their advice, it is no wonder that simplistic explanations of the entire phenomenon—concepts readily understandable by a sixth-grader—might be viewed as heretical.

I stand by all my analogies, however simplistic. Downsizer Bill Dunn, meet downsizer Bob Stempel.

In terms of financial strategy, the only meaningful difference in what the two have done is the number of zeroes involved.

18

When Liquid Is Solid

Remember all those colorful property deeds in the Monopoly board game? The red of Indiana Avenue, the green of Pennsylvania Avenue, the high-priced blue of Boardwalk?

When a Monopoly player gets greedy and wants to buy yet another hotel for one of his "developed" properties, he "mortgages" one of his other mythical holdings and picks up a shot of cash from the bank. The mortgaged property's colorful deed must be turned downward on the table to show that it is useless. If an opponent's token lands on a mortgaged square, he sees the black-and-white, belly-up notice of indebtedness, and knows he is home free.

Watching the '80s roll by in the real world was like watching a giant Monopoly game. The players leveraged themselves into a position where they owned many pieces of paper and not much else. Debt service soared to meet revenues somewhere in the clouds.

An old credit hand could only stand by and watch in amazement, offering advice that seemed as out of step with the times as wing-tipped shoes.

As the '80s neared the end of their overheated course at the credit windows, I wrote two articles headlined "Bracing for the Downturn" and "Trouble for the '90s." I predicted that the '90s would be an extraordinarily good time to buy a used yacht. That prediction is coming true; my main point, of course, had nothing to do with nautical bargains. I knew that the '90s would usher in a strong upturn in my consulting business, that a lot of companies would be in serious trouble. Too many principals were treating liquidity as an unknown or obsolete concept.

The '80s were good times, you will recall. On paper, a lot of companies made a lot of money.

Principals of small to medium-sized companies, people who receive the mail at a large percentage of our finest suburban addresses, extracted enormous amounts of cash from their firms for personal use. Besides yachts, expensive cars and ever-more expensive educations for their children, they purchased—or, rather, made down payments on—fine second homes in exotic locales. That is, after all and reportedly, the last remaining tax shelter.

Many of these entrepreneurs also unloaded drawers of cash on business expenditures that might have appeared, on the surface, to be the right and proper capitalist thing to do. They bought other businesses just as leveraged as theirs—and then leveraged them again. Sometimes they tied up cash in a second manufacturing plant—one in just as bad shape as their original golden goose. They bought vacant industrial-zoned real estate for future and vague or unrealistic expansion. Or, confidently riding a half-dozen straight years of profits, they plunged further into debt to upgrade or expand their equipment.

What's wrong with that? You invest, you prosper, the growth improves the lot of your employees. Well, investment and capitalism are indeed virtues. But even virtue can run amok on future dollars.

What's missing in this picture is liquidity. That means flexibility, the *ability to respond to crisis*. Without liquidity, you are like an outlaw sauntering into town with a noose already around your neck. The party might last a *very* long while; but when somebody finally yanks that rope, you have no recourse but to swing in the breeze and briefly contemplate what might have been.

In one of my 1989 articles, I noted one consequence of the long up side of the business cycle: the emergence of a number of business owners who had never encountered the growth and educational privilege of weathering bad times. The only scenario these youngsters had witnessed was tidy and lucrative: You put money in the pipeline, and a larger sum comes out the other end. If that indeed were a realistic script, the only logical course would be to stuff every penny you could borrow into the pipeline. Even Hollywood, however, would recognize that as unbelievable hogwash. "Next time," any producer would tell the would-be scriptwriter, "go for a little realism."

Living in the Future, as you saw in our discussion of personal finances, is the antithesis of realism. In the corporate world, where cash flow and paper assets get truly serious, the ability to amass unrealistic debt challenges comprehension.

One of the great verbal ironies of my business is that *liq-uid*ation is the term applied when a company departs the face of the Earth. I would have been present at these burials far less often if the principals had maintained their ability to do a little selective and voluntary *liquid*ating of their own—if they hadn't already buried themselves in debt.

The troubled company does not become troubled because it doesn't know how to make what it makes or do what it does. The troubled company is one that has had its good days, so it must have been doing something right. Its yesterdays included some bright and shining moments. But today is the tomorrow it didn't anticipate—the one that dawned cloudy and gray.

Every company, of course, has days like that. But not all of them get into serious financial trouble. Why is that? Usually it's because the solid company has a cushion, has flexibility, has some options, and is able to take swift action. It can shut a plant, it can sell unencumbered and unneeded assets. It can downsize and, at the same time, increase working capital. These are not ingenious responses to hard times. They are simple and logical steps, but they are not available to a company that is highly leveraged and living far into the future.

When the cash flow becomes a trickle, that unfortunate

company's receivables—probably one of its largest assets—already are pledged to the bank. Its machinery and equipment are so heavily mortgaged that liquidating some of those assets would accomplish nothing except to reduce total debt. Its buildings and the land they sit on are similarly pledged and useless. What this company needs more than anything is cash. But even if it cannibalizes itself and reduces expenses, it cannot raise a penny.

This company has borrowed itself into total inflexibility and strangled itself on the future. When the cash was rolling in, the principals either took it out of the company to buy personal toys or they invested it in something illiquid—rather than reducing debt. They projected a successful year into many successful years to come. But when things slowed in January, got slower in February, and got even slower in March, the company's debt service was still at December's levels. And in April, credit managers of the company's suppliers would hear: "I can't pay."

Often that occurs shortly after the overextended principals discover, the hard way, that a bank is not a pawn shop. They make the false assumption that because their balance sheet indicates assets are much greater than liabilities, they can march off to the bank and take another step into the future. Banks, however, are not interested in acquiring companies at bargain basement prices. They are interested in being repaid. Banks want to know why, if the company can't service the existing debt, it will be able to handle an even bigger debt service in the future.

To a lender, our struggling principals learn, collateral is only as good as the cash flow that supports it. Banks are not interested in lending money to support losses. They are interested in collateral for purposes of security, not for purposes of repayment.

This is the classic business trap of Living in the Future.

When you leverage yourself to the degree that everything you own remains illiquid, it is nearly impossible to get liquid again. If your company is losing money and you need cash to support the losses, good luck. You are in the midst of a most serious financial crisis.

If your company is losing money—and even if you hold substantial assets free and clear—the lending institution will require proof that they will be repaid before they will write you a check.

Even if you hold an *unusual* percentage of land and buildings and equipment free and clear, and even if you are not living far into the future, you will incur substantial losses either by borrowing money or selling assets during hard times—when your assets will be substantially worth less, if you're lucky. If you are unlucky, you won't be able to sell that 100 acres of undeveloped land or that air-conditioned warehouse at any price. The suggestion, if I may be so bold, is that there is merit to that good, gray, aging entity known as "cash reserves."

There is a big difference, however, between a company being hurt and a company being in a serious financial crisis. Everybody gets hurt in business from time to time, including the most successful companies.

In a serious financial crisis, the most troubled companies have lived so far into the future that they have no idea where Point A is and cannot reach Point B under any circumstances.

If it's all that simple, surely not very many companies experience financial crisis? Or the ones that do are woeful enterprises? Or the people running them must be awfully stupid?

The answers are: "No." And "no." And "very seldom."

Few in number? Many troubled companies these days take their best shot at survival through an out-of-court reorganization, with the cooperation of their creditors. Even out of court, the end result can be liquidation. Formal bankruptcy, through the court system, generally means that the company's troubles run so deep that creditors forgo their best chance at 100 or 90 or 50 cents on the dollar in order to get first in line for any cents on the dollar. Count the formal bankruptcies in your local financial newspaper. It is a large and growing number, and represents only a shadow of the national picture.

Woeful enterprises? You would not have to step far back in

time to be considered mad for predicting that Eastern Airlines would amount to nothing more than a tear in Eddie Rickenbacker's eye. Or that venerable Macy's would need court protection from the pleadings of its vendors. I can assure you that in the realm of lesser-known manufacturers, retailers and service providers, most victims of Living in the Future once manufactured their goods or offered their services with the same pride and reputation as their more famous cousins.

Stupid people at the helm? Rarely do stupid people wind up in control of companies turning over several million dollars a year. Some do have brighter bulbs than others—but that can be said of brain surgeons, foundry workers and presidents of the United States. Some troubled principals are better motivated than others, usually from having built the company in question with their own hands. Generally, however, the phenomenon of Living in the Future entirely transcends issues of intelligence.

Walk into a fine restaurant in Ann Arbor or Georgetown or Cambridge. Notice the entrees and side dishes and desserts that derive 40 percent or more of their calories from fat. Notice the physics professor lifting the fork to his mouth. Is he *stupid*? The lifeblood of a business gets sucked into debt service the same way a physics professor's arteries get clogged: intemperate behavior by someone who should, and almost certainly does, know better. The lobster Newburg and the state-of-the-art phone system and the custard torte and that new factory down the street look just too good to resist. Waiter! Put them all on my tab—plastic, please.

Yes, improbable as it seems, Living in the Future is the ultimate reason that companies finally come to someone like me. Bad luck, changing times, an untimely work stoppage—any number of setbacks you can think of—*can* and *do* hurt a company. But a company that is not burdened by unrealistic debt usually can deal with its problems.

Companies that are buried in debt lack the flexibility to do so. Like a reckless Monopoly player, they can boast of owning Park Place and Boardwalk but they can't even pay their utility bills.

19

Haze on the Bottom Line

The balance sheet is one piece of the business world that has made its way into everyday popular parlance. The least sophisticated citizen in the land is fond of referring to "the bottom line." If he knew what a shifting piece of sand the bottom line really is, he probably wouldn't dream of using it as his phrase of choice to suggest something solid and irrefutable.

Net worth—what's left after subtracting a person's or company's liabilities from assets—is not a fact. It is an assertion.

If the assertion is true, then a good net worth is a fine and valuable thing—at least for the moment. If the assertion is false, then a good net worth is just another lie.

For example, troubled companies that do not meet their problems head on, or are incapable of doing so, often prostitute themselves by laying a phony assertion on a banker's desk. "I need working capital," the troubled principal will say, "and as you can see, the company has *a very good net worth.*"

What the banker is not being told is that the balance sheet includes a $1-million receivable, and a few smaller but significant ones, that will never be collected. The reason the money won't be collected is irrelevant. The point is, if this desperate principal had walked in the banker's door and said, "I have a million dollars sitting at home on my dresser," he would not be any less truthful.

That common little scenario illustrates just one of the thousands of situations that make all the cliches about business being a matter of "people" and "trust" and "confidence" and "reputation" absolutely true. It has taken me, for example, three decades to build a nationwide reputation as a straight shooter. When a client has a legitimate and honest shot at survival, and a good plan to do so, I explain that to a creditor or a banker and they usually listen. That reputation is my firm's single most valuable asset. Just where you put *that* on a balance sheet, I'm not certain.

At any rate, when a potential client brings me his version of a balance sheet, I spend about one minute looking at the liabilities. These are debts, and they are not going to change. Come back tomorrow and you'll see the same numbers. The rest of my study time—whether 15 minutes or 15 hours—I devote to the company's assets. That's where the sands shift quicker than on a windy day in the Sahara.

A wealthy individual, for example, might have a net worth of $40 million on assets of $140 million (including $3 million in cash) and liabilities of $100 million (debt tied up in real estate investments). If you are remotely acquainted with the savings and loan crisis, and what that did to the assets side of many balance sheets, you know what happened to such individuals. Without writing one check or moving one penny, they woke up one day and found they couldn't afford to put gas in their Mercedes. So we are not talking only of trickery and nefariousness. The assets side of the most honest and professional balance sheet is a mine field. Cash is cash. Any other asset is a maybe, a positive number whose real value depends upon ability and willingness of customers to pay their bills, upon shifting real estate markets, upon obsolescence, upon changing regulatory rules and tax laws—upon scores of factors, always including the "business climate." Over the years, both in credit management and after presiding over scores of liquidations, I have developed a particularly acute professional skill in translating these columns of assets into their current realities. And I can tell you that I have *never* encountered a situation where the estimates and assertions in the assets column were pessimistic.

When a potential client comes to me, balance sheet in hand, his company is usually out of control.

It might be totally insolvent, allowed to drift so far into the future that there is no hope of ever paying the bills, even at 50 cents on the dollar, and trying to get back on course.

Very often, however, a company is only seemingly insolvent. In actuality, it is *illiquid*. Even after filtering any nonsense or optimism out of its list of assets, it has a good net worth. Its assets total well above its liabilities. But it cannot pay its bills. By any realistic definition of the word, the company is *bankrupt*. Companies, and people, can be bankrupt because they're illiquid. It happens all the time.

The company usually has not been operating successfully for a year or two, whether because of bad management decisions or because of a downturn in the business cycle. Living in the Future has left the company illiquid and inflexible, and desperate measures often have been taken before the principal sought professional advice. The taxing authorities, for example, may be lurking outside the door (and wielding a very big stick) because the business, desperate for cash, has dipped into withholding funds to meet overhead.

Banks or other major lenders are aware of what is happening, and know that the value of the company's assets are continuing to erode. A bank might say, "We agreed to loan you a maximum of $1.5 million against 80 percent of eligible receivables. Well, we're now shrinking that to 60 percent." And usually the company already has borrowed the full 80 percent—meaning that any money coming in must go toward reducing the bank balance.

Suppliers, without whom the company cannot get through the day, are on the phone wanting to know when they will be paid. What they hear is some of the most creative dialogue this side of Hollywood.

So here sits the principal of a company that has a positive net worth but no working capital, couldn't pay its bills yesterday and will have even greater trouble paying them today because the bank has reduced its line of credit. His world is crumbling around him, but most of the time—despite the desperate situation—he will point to his balance sheet and seek to give it an optimistic spin.

"Look," he'll say, "at all those assets. There's a way out of this, right?"

Maybe. Maybe not.

The first thing we have to do is generate our own version of a balance sheet, a three-dimensional report that analyzes all three of the worlds where businesses live: the past, the present and the future.

Then, if the business indeed still has a future, we'll try to reel it back into the present so it can get there.

20

The Real Bottom Line

I strive to be a troubled business's rescuer, not its mortician. Sometimes, however, there is no choice but to order crepe instead of confetti. When a client walks in the door for the first time, an hour or two of conversation and study usually give me a pretty good idea which it will be. But I take no action and utter no strong opinion until I have studied The Report.

That's not a formal title, of course. But it has become such an ingrained part of our operation that it might as well be. "Not until I see The Report" is common response to an inquiry from a client in the first few days of an engagement.

Launching this analysis is the very first step of every case we take on. Meanwhile, inquiring creditors are informed that we have been engaged, that The Report is being compiled and will be completed shortly—usually in less than a month. For the creditors, it's a good-news, bad-news message; mostly it's good. Confirmation that my client is in trouble is bad, but it's not really news; the creditor was the first to know. The fact that my firm has been retained is good news. The creditor knows that a dispassionate assessment will be made, and no one will be saying "your check is in the mail" unless it is.

My associates, with access to the company's books and records and after extensive discussion with company management, produce a document designed to give a clear and concise picture of *where the company has been* (typically the past five years of operation), *where it is now* (typically the most recent 30 days), and *where it will be at a realistically projectable point in the future* (typically six to 12 months).

Past, present and future add up to reality, and understanding.

Analyzing the past allows you to take a look at the level of expenses and income at a time when the company was, hopefully, operating profitably. Then, when you examine where the company is now, you will discover in every case that income is down dramatically—but expenses are either at the same level or, if they have been reduced, have not been reduced proportionally.

Next you must make a *realistic* estimate, based on both internal realities and external forces, of where the company's volume and income will go over the next 12 months. Any analysis further into the future is a meaningless crystal-ball act. What we usually see is that foreseeable future income will be closer to current levels than to what it was in the past.

If the company, however, is not too far buried in debt, and if it has a viable product or service, and if it has a customer base that will sustain some level of operations, it also has some options. Only these three simple options really count, however, and the company finally is about to meet them face-to-face: increase income, reduce expenses, or do both.

There is usually little we can do to increase a company's income, because there is not much that the company itself has not already tried. Often a struggling principal, who got into trouble in the first place by projecting past successes into the future and borrowing heavily on them, clings stubbornly to the idea that nothing is wrong that cannot be cured by a few flips of the calendar. When a potential client says, "I'm in a real bind but my sales are going to climb in the next 12 months," I'll take a careful look at our analysis. Most likely I'll be forced to say, "I don't know what world you're living in, but we don't think your sales are going to improve to a degree that would even approach solving your problem."

Obviously, the only thing we have to work with is the company's expenses. In essence, it is my sad duty to tell the client: "Here's your income now, and here's your $2 million loss for the last 12 months. If you don't want another $2 million loss 12 months from now, what does that tell you we have to do? We're going to shut down one of your plants, and 90 percent of those people will have to go. We have to sell some machinery and equipment. We have to lower your expenses in proportion to your lowered income."

And further: "We have to have a business plan based on these realities, with no subterfuge or phony projections, so we can convince your creditors not to seal your fate in an even worse package."

That is why our logo says "management and *adjustment* consultants." We adjust debt and adjust expenses. It's like going to a financial chiropractor. We do some very professional cracking, pulling and twisting. Anyone would expect the need for that exercise with the creditors, who are understandably eager to be paid. As you will see in the next chapter, the client himself often needs a fair amount of pulling and twisting into the present.

The goal, ironically, is to buy a little more of the future for our client. No matter how solid his new business plan, no matter how many economies will be made to survive, he needs some time or he will fail. The key step in the most massive corporate debt restructuring you can imagine is a high-powered version of young Bill Dunn sitting down and writing to his department store creditors. The stakes are huge, rather than puny, and the creditors are far less disposed to benign acceptance of a plan. The principle remains the same: An honest, well-drawn plan for extracting a debtor from Living in the Future—with realistic prospects of success, and properly executed—offers the best possible solution for all parties to the problem.

Pitfalls must be negotiated, however, which Bill Dunn never dreamed of.

Creditors of distressed companies will not be happy, no matter how masterful and honorable a plan is devised. At best, they will get their cash—sometimes very large sums of cash—late. That is not going to make anyone happy. Quite possibly they will get less than 100 cents on the dollar. Such a settlement will be more than if the company is forced into liquidation, but that is usually not going to make anyone happy.

We are also striving for an out-of-court reorganization, because the vast majority of companies that seek to right themselves within the burdensome bankruptcy system do not emerge from the process. However, any three creditors with claims totaling more than $5,000 may petition for an involuntary bankruptcy. And that does happen, even when the exasperated creditor would have been better off to accept the out-of-court plan. The larger the number of creditors, the more likely that three of them, for whatever reason, will seek an involuntary.

Some creditors sit in a better position than others. An anxious first secured creditor, for example, may insist on salvaging what he can from an immediate liquidation rather than awaiting the outcome of our new business plan. When such trump cards are played, often you must fold and walk away.

If a taxing authority holds access to a big enough chunk of a company's assets, and if it is indifferent to the well-being of my client *or* his creditors, then all may be lost.

So there is untold cracking, pulling and twisting to be done.

Without that dispassionate analysis in the first days of an engagement, and the business plan derived from it, however, there would be no chance for adjustment at all. The Report is the X ray that tells us where to begin, or whether to begin at all. And it is the foundation for building trust among the creditors. At the moment they are wolves at the door; but unless they are transformed into partners, however reluctant, the plan is doomed before it begins.

21

A Company in Trouble, a Person in Trouble

So who are these *people* who hire me, who anxiously await our analysis and then our prognosis? After all, I have said that I'm a numbers man and a credit man, but that I take great pride in paying close attention to the human side of these situations. Meanwhile, I have talked about materialism and about business owners who boldly reach as far into the future as their creditors will allow, and who—even with the cards all laid out on the table—are reluctant to admit they're holding a loser's hand. That doesn't sound very empathetic, I hear you say.

Wrong. With exceptions.

On a few occasions, mainly while functioning as a bankruptcy trustee, I have come upon situations where companies were raped by crooks. One of the most brazen of this lot was charged and convicted in federal court in 1991. No empathy there, of course.

On more than a few occasions, as a consultant, a client has turned out to be less than remorseful of his own contributions to a classic financial mess, and less than concerned about the havoc it will cause in the lives of others. Not much empathy there, either.

But the vast majority of my clients are *victims* of Living in the Future. They meant good, not harm, for their employees when they launched that expansion plan, however ill-advised it might have been. They didn't *plan* to stiff any creditors; things just started heading in that direction. They certainly didn't *plan* to lose their business, at worst, or at best to see it shrink while weathering a hellacious storm. Their greatest sin usually is the cornerstone of Living in the Future and the cartoon version of the American Way: They believed that every tomorrow would be better than the one before. Now they are paying the price.

Still doesn't sound very empathetic?

First of all, pain is pain and I don't like to see anyone endure it. I especially do not like to see someone in pain because of Living in the Future. It evokes memories of when I suffered the same pain.

Second of all, the reason I am able to help people is that I tell it exactly like it is. Anyone who comes to me to hear what they *want* to hear will leave sorely disappointed. If the malady in question were cancer rather than financial trouble, the client's only remaining alternative would be a practitioner in Mexico dispensing peach-pit extract. That's because I diagnose financial malignancies, expertly and frankly, and determine whether surgery would require removal of so many diseased organs from the company's body that it could not survive in any case. My office is the last stop. I never see my "patients" when they are well. They don't come to me and say, "Gee, Jim, we only made $4 million last year; what can we do to increase that?" They come to me and say, "Gee, Jim, we lost $4 million last year, the bank won't give us any more money, and our suppliers won't send us any more paper clips. What do we do now?"

I'm sure that a cancer surgeon telling a patient he is going to die has empathy for the patient. A doctor probably doesn't lecture the terminal victim about the evils of alcohol or tobacco or cholesterol. Nor do I take a client who is about to liquidate his business into a conference room and deliver a sermon on materialism, Living in the Future and a society that has overdosed on credit. My observation, however, is that doctors who spend hours, often futilely, trying to save lives that are being lost to behavior-induced disease often become fanatics for *prevention*. They become so frustrated with the suffering they see that, in effect, they devote their spare time in an effort to dry up their own customer base. So it is, in a way, with this book.

I have genuine empathy for my clients, and for their pain. I suffer with them all. I do everything possible to help them. When it works, if a restructuring is successful, the company survives and lessons are learned. If the damage is too great, we help the company die with dignity. Either way, cancer surgeons and turnaround specialists do not see a lot of repeat business. That is, not from the same clients. I do see the same situations, the same debt structure, the same mistakes time and time again. That is why I am painting this picture. Think of it as a preventive medicine poster.

Now, back to the question: Who are these people? For one thing, the principal of a troubled company that is headed for bankruptcy and gaining speed often is the loneliest man in the world. Surrounded by entreating people—employees, creditors, a dependent family—he nonetheless feels isolated on an island of debt. He feels, quite simply, like he is dying a very solitary death. The classic throwaway overstatement, "I'm so embarrassed I could die," is in his case neither throwaway nor overstatement.

How can *embarrassment* be so powerful?

Materialism. The lifestyle and social status a company provides in good times are substantial. Many, if not most, troubled principals simply cannot contemplate life without them. Moralistic judgment aside, this can be a fatal *business* mistake. An owner who continues to draw serious cash from a cash-poor company might as well throw a match in the fuel tank. Even if that is not the case, even if the personal lifestyle is being maintained on the principal's overheated personal plastic, the charade can cost him his company. Because even though this is a financial crisis, the real hard currency is *time*. Every day that the owner delays facing up to the problem, he diminishes the likelihood of solving it.

Postponement, however, is a specialty of most financially troubled businessmen. They are wrapped—trapped—in that false persona of materialism and status that can be maintained only as long as the factory or office is humming. After all, members of the principal's country club—and perhaps even his own family—define him as a guy who knows how to manufacture plastic-extruded doorknobs with greater profits than anyone in the business. The people he sees away from the factory also define him as the guy with the Mercedes and the Rolex who's in Garibaldi's every Friday night for the scampi, the one whose kid is at Harvard Law. Or so, at least, goes his perception of how others see him.

Bad times at the factory threaten this hard-earned personal mosaic. Embarrassment—not wanting to be defined as "the guy who put his kid in Central State when the factory got in trouble" —prevents action. Embarrassment and the effects of inaction place the factory closer and closer to bankruptcy. Denial sets in. In the extreme, the owner stays in his office behind closed doors. Or, incredibly, he takes a long golfing vacation in Florida. He clings to one thing: the near-pathological hope that, like a childhood beast in the night, his company's troubles will go away with a new dawn.

This is a stereotype, and my observations are not scientific; but they are real. Science would demand observing a control group who do *not* define their lives by the trappings of success, by an uninterrupted upward curve in lifestyle, who are not reluctant to take a few steps backward after so many leaps forward, who are not crippled by the embarrassment of it all. Such entrepreneurs, however, usually do not wind up on my doorstep. Perhaps an unscientific conclusion can be drawn from that fact.

The precious time that is wasted, measured in two ways, will determine the troubled company's fate.

First, how quickly the company says, "Enough!" How soon it stops the bleeding. How soon it tightens the belt and starts living in the present.

Second, how much time can be bought for the turnaround. Because no matter how good the recovery plan, it must be sold to the creditors. And then—*perhaps* after securing some new working capital—a long period of living staunchly in the present will be necessary to clean up the mess.

This second element—buying time and reorganizing—is up to specialists like myself. The first element lies entirely in the hands of the lonely, agonized and embarrassed principal.

Remember, we are not talking about a fatal instant's hesitation. Financial crises build over a *long* period of time. The wonders of credit being what they are, there is a substantial lead time from the first moment a business has trouble paying its bills to the time the IRS comes to padlock the door. That first moment is when an owner should seriously consider getting help.

Instead, a great many of my initial conversations with potential clients, long after a problem first surfaces, begin something like this:

Entrepreneur—"I can't pay my bills."

McTevia—"No wonder. You're buried in debt."

Entrepreneur—"I can't pay my bills because my bank won't lend me any more money."

McTevia—"Well, if I were your bank, I wouldn't lend you any more money, either."

22

A Bad-News, Bad-News Proposition

Not long ago I was engaged by a troubled Michigan manufacturing company. We'll call it AccuMax, which is not an attempt to be mysterious or cute. Legal, professional and moral constraints prevent me from identifying most of the clients whose stories, both successes and failures, go furthest toward illustrating the tale of Living in the Future.

The owners of AccuMax, with about 200 employees manufacturing and selling products to a market segment mired in a lengthy slump, did not call on me as a mortician. AccuMax had been in business for more than 45 years. Its products were excellent. The company, except for a relatively recent and ill-timed expansion, was doing nothing differently than it had during its very best times. The principals fully expected to remain in business, to be pillars of the community, to draw excellent salaries, to drive fine cars to the plant each day and be able to say: "Look at this: I've got the good life. And thanks to my company, all these people are making a living, too." The only problem with that scenario is that AccuMax was wallowing in debt, with no real sign of an end to a three-year revenue nosedive during which the company had charged forward—counting on a tomor-

row that would be better than today. Like thousands of companies, it was operating in the future while dwelling on its past
and remaining quite out of touch with its present.

The meeting during my initial analysis, at which the AccuMax principals would decide whether to engage my services,
unwound much like scores of other such meetings. Denial began
to be stripped away as the owners comprehended the magnitude
of their problem and the hurdles, perhaps insurmountable,
standing in their way. That is not entirely a drumbeat for my
powers of explication: Remember, the troubled businessman
does the summoning. Nothing happens until he picks up the
phone, a critical element of timing that lies entirely in his
hands.

We sat down one afternoon and talked for $3^1/2$ hours: the
two Accumax principals, their CPA and myself.

These initial meetings must especially be an exercise in
complete honesty, with no posturing and no mealymouthed ex-
changes. I try to signal that fact in all ways, big and small. So
even though in the initial minutes of a meeting I am likely to
be sized up as yet another visitor peddling his services, I pointed
out that I cannot stand tobacco smoke—and requested that one
of the principals refrain from smoking and that the gathering
be moved from a small office to a larger conference room.

During a tour of the plant, a glance at boxes and labels
had revealed the identity of some of AccuMax's major suppliers. So in the chit-chat before we got to the conference room, I
remarked to one of the owners that he must be dealing with
so-and-so and so-and-so—several credit people I knew on the
suppliers' staffs.

"You know so-and-so?" the principal asked.

"Yes, he used to work for me."

By the time we sat down, one of the principals had remarked that I must have been in the same kind of business as
AccuMax at some time. I told him I had not, but had been engaged by similar firms. To all of them I said: "I'm not a young
man anymore. I've been in this field a long time."

Sounds like a sales pitch? Yes, indeed. But my target is

their ears, not their wallets. What I was about to say to this small group, based on a phone conversation and a quick look at AccuMax's books, absolutely required that they believed I knew what I was talking about. Otherwise, they would not hear a word of it. Unlike most any salesman you can imagine, in the next few hours I did not tell these three men a single thing they wanted to hear.

"Before we get into this," I began, "I have a few things to say. I want you to know where I'm coming from, because I'm coming from an entirely different set of circumstances than anyone you ever have talked to before. What I do for my livelihood is so specialized that you have probably never talked to anyone like me. I'm going to say some things that are utterly shocking and strange to you."

"I want you to understand I realize that because you are not paying anything for today's meeting, you may think that what I'm telling you is not worth anything. That's up to you."

That's a fairly standard introduction. Next, I want to put myself in the potential client's shoes, and determine what I would do if it were my own company. To do that, I need to know more about the circumstances. So the four of us went through the financial condition of AccuMax, did a rough liquidation analysis—and estimated that if the company went out of business, its bank would barely get paid off. That, however, was only the bank. Several million dollars worth of creditors, and the people who owned the company, would get nothing at all!

I put the paper and our computations down on the table and asked: "Why do you want to keep this company going one more day? Do you think you can make this company profitable after losing millions in the last few years?"

The younger principal said he thought it could be done.

I said, "OK, what are you going to do differently tomorrow than what you are doing today."

"Well . . . " and he gave a response that roughly boiled down to a prediction that things would be better in the future.

"Let's look at this objectively," I said. "Pretend that you can pull all kinds of strings. That you can make major reductions in the payroll—cut out maybe 150 jobs. That I can tell your bank that you aren't going to pay the $9 million you owe, but if the bank freezes AccuMax's debt service for a year it eventually will be paid. That I can go to the $4 million worth of unsecured creditors and convince them to grant you a similar freeze."

"Now we have a snapshot," I told them, "of a business where everything is frozen. The bank is owed all this money, the creditors are owed all this money, and all you are gaining from the freeze is a chance to operate for a year under an interest moratorium while paying only for your current goods and services."

Then I reminded them that the working capital necessary to get from here to there meant someone would have to come up with *cash.*

I said: "If you owe a supplier $500,000 and tell the supplier that a push will put you in bankruptcy, that you want a chance to continue operations while paying cash up front—then that supplier will want to know where that cash is coming from. It's not going to come from the bank, we know that. It's not going to come from the creditors, we know that. That means it has to come out of *your* pockets, or you won't get from tomorrow until next year."

The principals mulled that stark fact and asked: "How much do you think we'll need?"

"It really doesn't matter," I said. "Let's ballpark it. Let's say you need a quarter of a million dollars. Are you willing and able to come up with a quarter million cash to take another year and see what you can do, as opposed to closing down?"

One owner quickly and confidently said: "Yes, I think I would do that."

"OK," I said, "I think that's dumb. What have you bought for $250,000? A year's time. Are you going to make a lot of money the following year? The best year this company has had in the last five barely equals the working capital you say you would raise and throw in—and we don't know if that is enough working capital. AccuMax has millions in debt. Do you know how long you have to operate this company at that level to pay millions in debt? Your kids and their kids will still be paying for it."

The reality of Living in the Future was setting in.

I told AccuMax's owners that they needed to develop a realistic picture of where the company has been, where it is, and where it is going; that they had to find out whether $250,000 would be enough to buy a year's time on the premise that the following year, finally, would dawn better than the one before. And if it really *is* $250,000 that's needed, did they want to raise it, or did they want to do the agonizing but logical thing and shrink the company down to prepare for liquidation? That would mean chopping payroll—including most of their own salaries and perks. In the best of all possible worlds, liquidation would lead to a buyer who valued at least some of the work force as part of the company's assets, and not everyone in the AccuMax family would have to go home broke.

This all transpired early in a meeting that began with the principals probably assuming, with their hearts if not their calculators, that somehow this company doctor would be coming along and administering a shot of penicillin that would get rid of the virus on their balance sheet.

In one shattering afternoon of conversation—a conversation I've had so many times that it's like seeing the same play performed repeatedly by different players—two troubled individuals moved a large part of the way from denial to reality. Not *all* the way. It's too big a step to be traversed that easily. But blunt talk diverts the desperate jugglers' gaze enough that they look at the ground and see how many balls already have fallen and scattered.

The likely impending death of a once vibrant and productive company is no less easy to comprehend than the death of a human you knew in his or her prime. Perhaps in the corporate world—where critical care usually is summoned and administered much too late—it's more difficult.

I told the AccuMax principals what I always say in cases of the most troubled companies. "Look, no matter what happens, the company may die but *you* will not die. You are smart guys. You are experienced. You will find something else to do. You may even be entrepreneurs again."

One owner very quickly said to me: "I may not die. But will I want to live?"

I told you I do not drag people in such situations into a closed room and lecture them on materialism. I don't have to. It's such an overriding part of the picture that the conversation just happens.

"Whether you want to live depends on what you perceive as the reason you're here on Earth," I told him. "If you perceive you're here to achieve much outward material success, if that is your measure, then you're in an excellent position to lose every-thing—at least for a while."

And I found myself thinking of an excellent piece written a few days earlier by a Detroit newspaper columnist, who said that the greatest way to measure success is by counting how many people miss someone when he or she is gone.

I said: "Do you have people who are going to miss you when you die?"

"I hope so," he said. "My wife loves me. So do my kids. Even my dog, I suppose."

"OK," I said, "then you have got to understand that you have some very important measures of success outside this com-pany. If you think this machinery is everything, you're kidding yourself. You're overreacting to a set of circumstances that are beyond your control."

We talked and, as is usually the case, he was interested and surprised that someone who pushes numbers around on paper was so in tune with the emotions of the moment. I cannot recall exactly what I told him, but it would have been from the portfo-lio of experiences you are now acquainted with. That I have suffered every pang of his agony. That I have never lost a com-pany, but I have been in tight enough spots to carry that anxious dread in my belly. And that, years ago, my personal finances were every bit as miserable as I suspected his were about to be. I didn't tell him about repo-ing cars and furniture; but—as al-ways—I told him he should not feel alone in his pain because I had seen it in enough faces to populate an incorporated village.

We agreed on a professional engagement. I sent my associates to prepare a report, to answer AccuMax's phones when creditors called, to let the wolves know that we were on the case. Perhaps the principals were still hopeful of a way out, of buying time for restructuring. But, as is usually the case, a sober analysis of the situation revealed it to be even further underwater than it appeared at first glance. Far enough that AccuMax was a company whose final time had come.

You cannot restructure a bowl of mortgaged Jell-O.

23

Corporate Death with Dignity

This is a book based on experience, not on research. So I cannot say whether a fur company or two, or perhaps an import-export company, has survived on these shores since before the Revolution. I doubt if a single commercial enterprise in Rome can trace its founding to the days of empire. I am most skeptical that any Cairo company can trace its lineage to the days of the pharaohs. With certitude I can say that Adam's haberdasher no longer sells fig leaves.

Companies pass through a life cycle, just as humans do. The principals endure phases of denial, anger and, hopefully, acceptance. And then the company is gone. Its demise might result from abuse, or it might be a natural death. A rapscallion principal might be squandering the profits, and then some, in Las Vegas. Or the most honest and efficient harness purveyor might be awakened one day by the ominous putter of a horseless carriage on the street. That happened in the Motor City, where my firm is based. Long forgotten is the fact that before Henry Ford, Detroit was the *kitchen stove* capital of the United States. Things change.

No matter why a company dies, it deserves—just like a human being—a peaceful and honorable death. It shouldn't disappear beneath a pack of wolves tearing at shreds of the carcass.

There should be no scavenging competition for the gold fillings in the corpse's teeth. The company should not be forced to go through bankruptcy. The survivors should grieve and move on, rather than endure an animalistic feeding frenzy. There is trauma enough in a peaceful passing. Then, at least, the people closest to the deceased are left with their dignity.

"Dignity" is a word I have heard a good many times from former clients whose companies were beyond saving. In paraphrase, they say: "McTevia, I paid you a lot of money. But let me tell you what you did. You left me with some dignity. And with that dignity I was able to go out and start this new life. You want to know something? I'm making more money than I was before. You were right. The company died, but I didn't."

The nature of my work is that I get a very close, internal look at several companies almost every week. Each of them represents the entire world for a person, or a few persons, who built and/or operate them. When I sit across the table from a troubled principal and study a line on his balance sheet, it must in a sense be much like a physician who peers through a weird little scope into a patient's stomach. The doctor is looking at some specific tissue with some specific properties and problems; but he is also looking—from an unusual perspective—at Fred, a nice guy who must get his son to a Little League game in an hour and a half and whose wife loves him very much but wishes he'd buy flowers more often.

How do you say, "I hope Fred Jr. hits a home run this afternoon. There's a special on red roses at Ajax Florist. And, by the way, your ulcer looks a little strange and I think we should do a biopsy"?

I have this ultimate advantage over the physician, however: I know that no matter what my prognosis for the client's company, there is no real reason he should die with it. And what I usually try to do is let them see that this entity they thought would go on forever is subject to the cycle of life. Just as you would expect, human beings who are nearest to completing their own life cycle tend to understand the concept best.

Many times I have sat at a table with several generations

of principals as a substantial family business met its ultimate fate. Recently I conferred with *four* generations of one family. Their business once provided a living for several hundred people and now was staggering toward the end with fewer than 20 employees, most of them relatives. We were peacefully liquidating the enterprise. The patriarch, in his 80s, understood perfectly.

"This company is more than 90 years old," I told him. "It has had some great times. It supported lots of families. It gave a lot to the community. This is still a *good* company. It has hung on long enough. If you keep going, it will be driven to the ground in bankruptcy. Shame on us if we let this once-proud company die that kind of death."

Why? Because companies that are not allowed to die timely and honorable deaths hurt people. Principals get hurt, and the people they do business with get hurt. When we arrive on the scene and do our analysis, what we are really doing—from this perspective—is determining whether a company is struggling for survival or merely struggling against the inevitable. There is a huge difference. If the principals could just remove themselves far enough from the situation, they could see the broad picture. We try to help them do that.

Companies struggling against the inevitable almost always wind up prostituting themselves. When the handwriting is on the wall, and the principal ignores it, he begins to prostitute himself, his associates, his employees. He has his people tell suppliers anything they want to hear so shipments will keep coming. He has his managers telling employees that everything is rosy—even though the employees know there isn't enough material coming through the door to keep the machinery going.

The principal himself paints rosy pictures to his banker. Perhaps he even does fraudulent things. He'll hide that bad receivable from his banker. He'll go home and convince his wife that everything is OK. Then she'll go out and buy a new coat, or a Mercedes, and he'll let her do that. When the kids want to go to an Ivy League school instead of junior college, he'll send them. He'll head for the country club and run up his credit cards.

He'll get himself into such a situation that when the inevitable happens, he will have completely destroyed his ability to survive emotionally and honorably.

When that scenario runs its ugly course, all of the people who worked with him will hate him, his bank will sue him, his wife will be faced with the fact that her husband wasn't honest with her, and the kids will announce that they would just as soon have had an honest junior college education. At the key moment, they all could have gone back and started over, working together. But that moment is lost forever.

That message I hear from old clients, that one about dignity? It isn't just moralistic. It's about getting on with a new life rather than destroying it. They go on to say: "In six months I was back in business, and some of the old employees came with me because I was so straightforward with them and did the best I could. Some of the key people came with me. My customers, my bank—I didn't do a number on them, and now they're willing to help. My wife? She's not wearing a fur coat, but she still loves me. I just couldn't see it, I was so wrapped up in this enormous facade."

A few years ago, the life cycle of companies brought a tremendous irony to my doorstep.

As a young man, it had been a pleasure and privilege to work for Peninsular Steel. It was a first-class company. It had no bank debt, carried substantial cash reserves, and had been very successful for two generations.

After I left Peninsular, economic conditions got tighter, and the market segment that this company once had all to itself became very competitive. Into the third generation of ownership, I was called in to take a look at Peninsular's situation. The new generation, in the style of the times, had purchased the firm through a heavily leveraged buyout. The previous generation took most of its money out of the firm and lived happily ever after. The new generation faced a bank with a first secured creditor position, bondholders (the former owners) in a second secured position, and a whole tier of unsecured creditors. The new generation shouldered an enormous debt that their predecessors did not, and were unable to pay it.

A company where I had learned so much about industrial credit, and where I had traveled far down the road to developing a free-lance consulting business in my spare time, had become a classic victim of Living in the Future. And now here I sat, at the Grosse Pointe Yacht Club, talking with its principals about the life cycle of companies.

I told them that Peninsular should die a proud death, that it should not struggle on into bankruptcy court, that they should not struggle to the ugly end while hoping for something to happen that wouldn't happen. It's about to be over, I said, and the only question is how to get it over in the most equitable and honorable fashion possible.

Liquidation is not a simple matter of hanging up an auction sign and counting the money in the cigar box at the end of the day. If Peninsular's liquidation were not done properly, not only would the unsecured creditors wind up with nothing, but the noteholders would be in serious trouble as well. We needed both the bank's and the noteholders' cooperation in not foreclosing, in keeping the case out of court. With some effort, we did so. Then we organized the other creditors and peacefully and as responsibly as possible disposed of Peninsular's assets.

It was one of the largest out-of-court liquidations I ever conducted. It involved millions of dollars, crossed several state lines and took a year and a half. The operating assets of the company eventually were sold, and many employees continued with the new company. We collected the receivables. A fine and proud company ceased to exist. Its bank got 100 cents on the dollar. Its bondholders got 100 cents on the dollar. Its creditors, who would have gotten nothing had the case gone to court, were paid about 60 cents on the dollar.

No struggling against the inevitable. No prostituting. Things change. Life goes on. Peninsular was not a bad company. It was a good company, and it died an honorable death.

As people rearranged their lives in the wake of the liquidation, there was even a bonus for McTevia & Associates. The credit manager who hired and trained me at Peninsular so many years ago signed on as a valued member of my staff.

Make no mistake about it: Business relationships are relationships between people, not between institutions. The language of our daily communications in the business world may well suggest otherwise. Whether it's engineering talk, or accounting talk or quality control talk, it can seem like so much jargon—dispassionate and abstruse—tossed back and forth in a setting of attache cases and appointment books. But the enduring bottom line involves people, integrity, reputation. And when a business winds down honorably, that is all preserved.

I say something like the following to every principal whose business is about to go away: "Not only are you not going to die when this company does—but the bank is not going to die, either. The bank's relationship has not been with this company; it has been with *you.* One of our jobs in winding down this company is to try to preserve that relationship—and all of the other relationships you have made in the business world. Because you are still going to be around when the last pallet has been auctioned. If you emerge from this situation with your integrity and reputation intact, you will have lost nothing but money."

It's a tough message to swallow. Some listen; some don't. It's just a case of choosing how to keep score.

24

The Black Hole

I have never known a leading physician in the treatment of dread "social" diseases. Nor have I known an executioner. I strongly suspect, however, that the pillars of any community are not eager to be seen in public with either. So it is that over the years Joan and I have led a fairly quiet social life. That has been partly by choice. But partly it has been because no one with a thriving business wants to be seen conversing at a corner table with a man who spends most of each day conversing with businessmen whose enterprises stand in grave danger of going in the tank.

This was particularly true in the early years of my consulting business, when a troubled company bore the stigma of a corporate leper. Corporate and personal financial attitudes, then as now, marched in lockstep. An individual or a company that didn't pay was a deadbeat. Any person or firm tainted with a mere whiff of bankruptcy was an outcast. When they called, I was one of the very few people answering the phone.

Times change.

Today, formal bankruptcies—personal and corporate— have soared, tripling in a half-dozen years, to levels once associated only with Great Depressions and social chaos. Newspaper stories report company restructurings in tones barely more pejorative than an item announcing that a new warehouse has been opened. A bad-news event that was rare has become a bad-news event that is routine. The average literate citizen, who once could not have told you a single specific about bankruptcy, can now give you a working definition of "Chapter 11." A legion of lawyers, accountants and consultants stand in line to service the accounts. And though my social profile remains low, I no longer quite feel like I am wearing a scarlet "B" at public gatherings.

You need to know just a bit about this swarm of bad-news bulls, and the now-crowded environment in which they—and I—operate. It's a generally ignored piece of the puzzle that reveals basic changes in the American way of life. It's also a window through which you can clearly see just how pervasive and pernicious Living in the Future has become.

When I came into the business in the early '60s, bankruptcy was an unusual event. It was not an acceptable way of solving problems. The fact that I was virtually alone in my field represents a sort of chicken-and-the-egg proposition. People were avoiding bankruptcy because it was not acceptable. At the same time, people, companies and our government generally were not so mindlessly Living in the Future. Which came first? Without clever analysis, let's just say that—at all levels—attitudes about financial integrity go hand in hand with levels of debt service.

An unusual confluence of events occurred in the late '70s. A serious business slump caused an increase in bankruptcies—and, of course, an increase in the number of practitioners to deal with them. At virtually the same time, the U.S. Bankruptcy Act was replaced by the Bankruptcy Code. The manner in which troubled companies dealt with their creditors would never be the same.

I began doing court work in the '60s under the old Bankruptcy Act, worked in the field during the transition to the Bankruptcy Code, and continue to work in the field today. The changes have been basic and huge.

For one thing, and to put a complex story in a context anyone can relate to, my rates have gone up. Where I was once a Lone Ranger credit man helping to clean up these messes of debt, I am now surrounded in the field by prestigious accounting and other professional firms. This—coupled with ever-rising demand—has dramatically increased prevailing professional rates in bankruptcy cases and in turnaround management. Fees in just the last 10 years have gone from $50-$100 an hour to $300-$350 an hour. The adage of making hay while the sun shines is not entirely inappropriate.

For another thing, the Bankruptcy Code established an entirely new federal bankruptcy bureaucracy. Bankruptcy referees were replaced by bankruptcy judges. Where "receivers" once were appointed, "trustees"—overseen by a new federal trustees office—are now assigned when necessary to each case.

Most importantly, the old Bankruptcy Act, in the vast majority of cases, placed an outside receiver squarely in charge of a troubled firm. But under Chapter 11 of the Bankruptcy Code, a reorganization now usually leaves the "debtor in possession" of his troubled company. The wisdom of this change remains a matter of considerable debate. On the one hand, some parties to these disasters—particularly, and obviously, many creditors—wonder what sense it makes to have a troubled company remain controlled by someone who got it in trouble in the first place. On the other hand, how much wisdom can be found in taking a company on the brink of failure and placing it in the hands of someone who doesn't know where the men's room is—let alone, for example, how to produce and market optical sensors for industrial robots?

This transition from one bankruptcy system to another involved a lot of uncomfortableness and a lot of turmoil. The fact that it coincided with the late-'70s recession only compounded the upheaval. As it turned out, the last drip of that flood of bankruptcies was just being mopped up as the most recent downturn struck.

What creditors and troubled principals discovered as the first batch of bankruptcies made its way through the new system was that this had become an extremely expensive way of solving a problem. The new level of bureaucracy added cost, as did the escalating fees of the practitioners. Creditors trying to extract payment for a shipment of steel or television sets or clothing saw red—lots of it, as in red ink—in the hourly practitioner fees that were being extracted first, off the top of the wounded debtor's carcass. Seeing hundreds of thousands—even millions—of dollars spent in bankruptcy expenses, they threw up their hands and said, "There has to be a better way of doing this."

There is a way, and it is my way—or at least my preferred way. Before the Bankruptcy Code I was doing 90 percent of my work in court. Now I do 90 percent of my work outside court. Out-of-court restructuring, the more sophisticated version of what young Bill Dunn did with his stack of bills, in my opinion is the most equitable and cost-efficient way of solving a company's problems. Assuming, of course, that they are solvable.

I have said here that business is a matter of confidence and trust. An out-of-court restructuring pushes confidence and trust to the outer limits. Confidence and trust already have been violated, or there would be no need for restructuring. The process requires summoning the final reserves of both commodities for one last attempt to avoid the vulture swarm in which my client firm would die, and in which very few creditors would get their just portion of satisfaction. A large part of my job is to evoke that final confidence and trust, that *credit*. The fact is, any confidence and trust I can find among the creditors tends to be directed to my own firm's presence on the scene rather than to my client. Fortunately, a good many pragmatic reasons exist for a creditor to sign on for an out-of-court restructuring.

First of all, no one wants to go to court for a Chapter 7 bankruptcy unless a company is so far underwater that nothing can be done but throw it in the recycling machine and hope that a few pennies of marketable scrap come out the other end. Chapter 7 means liquidation, not reorganization. And even liquidation, given a situation that is not totally out of control, can be achieved more peacefully and equitably out of court. Under Chapter 7, there is no creditors' committee, and these unfortunate souls have no real say in the outcome. They can go to court and scream, but for the most part the trustee will liquidate as he sees fit. In two or three or four years, the bureaucracy will have extracted its fees; what remains might not be worth re-trieving.

Second of all, a Chapter 11 bankruptcy—a restructuring under the aegis of the court—is expensive, time-consuming, laden with red tape and always in danger of being pushed into a Chapter 7 proceeding. This contributes to the fact that only a very small percentage of companies that attempt to reorganize under Chapter 11 do so successfully.

So I have more than goodwill on my side when I appear before a creditors' committee to say: "My client is in trouble, which you know all too well. We need your help—and some time—to stabilize the company and get it back on its feet." It is far, however, from an easy sell. It is always raucous, frequently impossible. A troubled firm's creditors are aggrieved people. Credit was extended, and all that is coming back in the mail is trouble. Only two emotions are logical in this setting: Frustra-tion and anger.

Skydiving and mountain climbing, I'm sure, have their mo-ments of exhilaration when the practitioner can feel that he has stepped into another dimension. But even after all these years, I doubt that stepping out the door of an airplane offers a greater sense of defying gravity than asking people who are owed mil-lions of dollars to show a little patience, to keep this situation out of court—and, by the way, perhaps to deliver a few more truckloads of supplies. The former requires audacity and a para-chute. The latter requires integrity, a well-gathered collection of cold facts, total understanding of where lie the best interests of every party to the disaster, and a plan that will lead the creditors to say: "This is a truly crummy hand, but I'm best off if I hold onto it and play it."

I think you now see more fully the importance of The Re-port. In those first few days after being called in by a troubled principal, *everything* depends on exposing an accurate reconais-sance photo of his business and precisely analyzing prospects and a path for digging out. In terms of who is paying the bill, we are preparing the analysis for my client. In practical, imme-diate terms of getting the job done, we are preparing the analysis for the legion of creditors without whose cooperation this company will be history. It is not a time for smoke and mirrors.

In essence, we call the troubled firm's creditors to a meeting, give them our analysis of the situation, tell them the new business plan that our client hopes to have an opportunity to execute. If we have had time for a full investigation of the situation, we assure them that there has been no fraud, and there have been no preferences in paying debt. Lacking time, we tell them that we'll have those assurances in a matter of days. Preference and fraud, by the way, are in my opinion the only reasons that a company should be pushed into bankruptcy court. As a matter of professional responsibility, and as a practitioner who serves as a federal bankruptcy trustee, if I discover the existence of either, it will duly be reported.

We answer the creditors' questions, but first we try to paint such a complete picture of the client's situation that not many questions remain. No one, for example, will have any illusions about the existence of untapped assets within reach of the creditors. We then ask them to study our analysis, to form a committee, and to tell us if they come to the same conclusions that we have. If so, we start the process of restructuring—or, if necessary, liquidating—out of court. If not, the case passes into the bowels of the bankruptcy system.

Sitting in the room and deciding which path will be taken are "the creditors"—meaning a few principals but mainly credit managers, financial officers or attorneys. In some cases they are learning for the first time that a receivable they thought to be good, and which they were responsible for extending, will be worth only 50 cents on the dollar. These are not happy people. My task is to make them de facto partners with the company that did them wrong.

The beauty part is that after handing them an honest analysis of the troubled company, I can stand up and say: "Listen, I have filled every role that is being played by a member of this creditors' committee. I've been a banker. I've worked for firms where I was the one who extended credit that turned sour. I have owned companies with receivables. And let me tell you, nothing ever made me more furious than to open a letter announcing that a customer had gone into bankruptcy. Why didn't they give me a chance to sit down with them and work something out?"

That is my professional goal: To avoid the black hole of bankruptcy wherever possible. Unfortunately, the nature of my profession is that my clients generally are hanging over the edge, by their fingertips, when I meet them.

25

The Greatest Thing Since Sliced Bread

Sometimes it all works. Right down to the last penny and the last check in the mail. Such are the unforgettable times—and I suspect it's the same no matter what your occupation—that you are glad you do what you do.

That is why I cannot look at a store-wrapped loaf of bread without thinking of a man we will call Bill Baker. Bill was a remarkable man, and a delightful one, to whom no one had ever said "no." As a result, Bill never could say "no," either. It nearly cost him everything.

As with most of my success stories, I cannot use real names. No one wishes the world to read how they once came within one payroll or one angry creditor of going belly up. The story of Acme Bread was a matter of excruciating embarrassment for Bill Baker, and a near-disaster for a substantial and well-known corporate citizen of a mid-sized Michigan community.

Acme Bread turned out its first loaf in the 19th Century. By 1980, when the company engaged my firm, its bread was sold by 1,900 dealers throughout southern Michigan. Annual sales had reached $11,000,000. The company, nonetheless, was near insolvency. Bill Baker seriously entertained an investment group's offer of $150,000 to walk away from this multimillion-dollar company founded by his grandfather.

The founder had worked long and hard to build the business. So had his son. Bill Baker, representing the third generation of bread purveyors, experienced the childhood blessing and curse of that hard-earned and considerable success. It was not Bill's fault that, as a child, he received an allowance and never really knew where it came from. Nor was it his fault that the bakery had *always* been there, as long as he could remember, and that *every* tomorrow—as far as he could see—would dawn better than the one before. Such is not the kind of background that allows painful decisions to be made.

When the founder's son died in 1954, Bill became president of the bakery. He lived in a grand style, with all the perks and prominence of a major local businessman. He treated his more than 300 employees well. Money always had flowed from the ovens like so much pumpernickel, and—to put a simplistic but fair slant on Bill's management style—Bill assumed that it would always be thus.

By 1980, after three straight years of losses, Bill was mulling the paltry offer of $150,000. Such a fire sale would allow him to escape the pain and embarrassment of watching it all go down. Perhaps the investment group would save the company by doing the agonizing things—like slashing overhead, cutting a new deal with the union, deferring payment to some creditors—that Bill did not want to do. Even late in life, knowing that the buyout would leave him with nothing in his remaining years, Bill thought that perhaps he would rather face that consequence than do the hard things that needed to be done.

My firm got involved because Bill's attorneys recommended us. I vividly remember driving over to Bill's home on a Saturday afternoon and pleading with him not to unload Acme Bread for a pittance. I also came to realize, almost immediately in what became a close friendship, that Bill's warmth and generosity—granted almost without question—were his greatest flaw as a businessman. Anyone who doubts that the personality of a principal is reflected in the personality of a company need only take a look at the situation of Acme Bread in 1980.

Administration and marketing departments were overstaffed, creating one bigger happy family—but ballooning the overhead. In-house vehicle maintenance had evolved into a cost-inefficient fiefdom. Accountability, both by departments and individuals, was foggy at best.

At that, Acme Bread might have plodded along as an inefficient underachiever in terms of profitability. But Bill—by nature a prime candidate for Living in the Future—had sliced open a financial artery by building one of the finest state-of-the-art automated baking lines in the central United States. It was a marvel to see, as it churned out enough bread to stock convenience stores and supermarkets from Detroit to Grand Rapids. Bill, however, had overlooked the fact that his underachieving cash flow would not nearly service the debt on this multimillion-dollar investment. Like an over-yeasted dough, it rose and spread across Acme Bread's bottom line. By the time I first talked to Bill, the company was staggering beneath its daily pile of bills, much like a typical overextended individual. Of its $750,289 in overdue payables, 187 had balances of less than $500!

With not one ounce of deceit, greed or nefarious motive of any sort, Bill Baker had led himself and his company to the brink. More than anything, he wanted not to be in charge when the walls came tumbling down. The bargain hunters knew a buyer's market when they saw one.

"Don't do it, Bill," I pleaded to him that Saturday. "Your company is worth much more than that. I don't know how much more—but a *lot*. Give me a chance to sort it out."

I use the word "pleaded" intentionally. Pleading for business is not my style. But the situation itself was begging for a turnaround effort. It would be an utter and classic shame if this fine man were left penniless, more out of generosity than anything else. Even before doing a complete analysis, it was obvious that—by making some tough, painful decisions—Acme Bread could be put back on its feet.

"The key thing," I told Bill Baker, "is that you'll have to step to the side during the restructuring. We can't have you going around playing Daddy Warbucks while I'm trying to save your company."

He came to the conclusion that he liked what I had to say, even though it included perhaps the most backhanded compliment he had ever heard. He signed an engagement letter. And he stepped aside so we could do the job.

I'm proud of our work over the following six months. There was nothing unusual in our approach, however. It followed the formula you are by now well-acquainted with. We bought time from creditors by showing them, honestly and completely, the company's position and our plan to get from Point A to Point B. We paid off the small debts first, in one quick flurry. Then we got on with timely repayment of restructured larger debt. We cut expenses by bringing much-needed economies to several segments of the operation. With a viable plan in place, we secured some new working capital. Some of the details would be interesting if this were a business text, which it is not.

This is the bottom line: In less than a year, the Baker family sold its company for nearly $9 million. Bill Baker, whose only sin was Living in the Future, was able to live out his remaining years without losing the status and comforts that always had been his, and which he had done nothing to taint. More important to Bill, I know, was the fact that he had not suffered the ultimate embarrassment of being the family member who finally killed the golden goose.

The painful financial decisions that Bill was unable to make are essentially the same as the millions of financial decisions that face all of us, from Bill Dunn's small personal budget to General Motors' new realities to those infinite and uncountable zeroes in our government's deficit. The near-humiliation encountered by as fine a man as Bill Baker is perhaps the greatest single illustration in my personal experience that the best-intentioned, most humane, most generous motives are not sufficient to sidestep the painful choices required of living in the real world. Those who attempt to sidestep those choices only invite chaos and a pain that is compounded many times over.

Over the years, I have tried to communicate this fact in one way or another in various articles and lectures to business groups. The avoidance of pain always has seemed to me to lie at the core of the serious financial difficulties I encounter. It does not take a genius to add up the numbers. And I'm sure I have risked scorn in some quarters by pointing out that reducing expenses and increasing revenues are the only way to solve a financial problem, speaking strictly in financial terms. It is precisely because the financial side of it is so ridiculously simple that I insist on injecting the human dimension into all these discourses on numbers.

In the late '70s I happened to pick up a copy of a best-seller titled *The Road Less Traveled,* by M. Scott Peck. I immediately recognized the similarity of Dr. Peck's theme to what I was observing in my professional life, and what I was trying to communicate about painful financial decisions.

In the first section of the book, Dr. Peck shows that problem-solving involves pain, and that the tool for solving problems is discipline. I began to incorporate this message in most of my articles, many of my lectures—and all of my professional engagements. I usually distribute copies of *The Road Less Traveled* to all of a seriously troubled company's principals and department heads. I tell them we are about to begin a long, painful journey along the road less traveled. I tell them they have been traveling the more popular, wide, seemingly easy road that reaches far into the future, robbing the company of flexibility and inviting financial disaster.

What we are talking about here, really, is not numbers but *problem-solving.* And resolving problems in personal life, in business, in communities and in government requires the same basic steps.

For me, it's a matter of convincing owners of companies that the old way of doing business is wrong, as comfortable as it may feel and regardless of whether competitors are conducting business in the old way. It's a process that must be stopped. Unfortunately, only companies that are in deep financial trouble, with their very survival in doubt, seem to have the incentive to begin the process.

It begins, of course, with discipline: the discipline of self-examination. Where has this company been over the last several years? Where is it today? And where, if current policies and procedures continue, will it be about a year from now? Only if the answer to the latter question is, "Out of business," does a company seem able to marshal the discipline necessary to make change. Why? Because of pain.

It is painful to confront one's family and inform them that a comfortable and familiar way of life must change. It is painful to tell one's business associates and employees that the old way of doing business is history. It is painful to shrink, or even disassemble, an organization that has grown beyond its financial capabilities. It is painful to confront suppliers and customers. Business owners usually take every step possible to avoid all this pain—*even in a situation where sixth-grade arithmetic points to the painful solution.* Such is the emotional reward our society confers upon growth and prosperity, and the shunning it confers upon openly admitted and addressed financial adversity. But this is the pain that Dr. Peck suggests always accompanies problem-solving.

Oh yes, honesty. It is, along with discipline, one of the cornerstones of problem-solving. No smoke and mirrors. Honest assessment of a financial situation. Trimming fat—and, if necessary, muscle—to make the marathon equation balance. Moving back from a dishonest and unrealistic step into the future. Enduring pain to get from Point A to Point B. Solving a financial problem.

Dr. Peck's book was not exactly an eye-opener for me. It was more a stunning—and eloquent—confirmation of truths that I had observed in every corner of my professional life. Problems that seemed to me not to be numbers problems, because the numbers were so damned simple, were indeed *not* numbers problems. They were problems of discipline, resolve and willingness to confront a problem and endure pain.

In the years since stumbling upon his book, I have met Dr. Peck and have talked with him many times, but I have never apologized for quoting him so often. He didn't say it first; he just said it better.

Bill Baker, who gave more to his community than 99.9 percent of mankind, faltered only because he lacked the discipline and willingness to endure pain, and thereby solve his financial problem. Because of that, he looked disaster square in the eye.

I wish I could have given him a copy of *The Road Less Traveled* about 20 years earlier.

26

Living Illegally in the Future

Statistically, Living in the Future is seldom a criminal enterprise. Charging a pound of hamburger and an eight-pack of Coke on your plastic probably ought to be a crime, but it isn't. As a laborer in the deepest recesses of unrealistic debt, however, I've encountered my share of instances where greed has escalated into criminal fraud.

Gathering and circulating knowledge that will help eliminate business fraud is one of the many goals of the National Association of Credit Management, an organization of commercial credit executives. As an old credit manager, and as a 30-year member of the association, I know that ever more clever fraudulent schemes—and some time-tested and proven chestnuts—are practiced far more often than the public realizes. Greed, and the morally bankrupt perception that white-collar crime is somehow less criminal than armed robbery, are powerful motives.

Decades ago as a repo man, I saw my share of small-scale fraud, as well as innocent misery. Buying consumer goods with no intention of paying for them is, after all, the blue-collar equivalent of white-collar crime. My youthful repo career brought me in touch with numerous shady doings—such as the suitcase loaded with white powder. But years after I last had to repossess a car in the dead of night, I ran into yet another situation illustrating how the various threads of this tale inter-weave at every level. The situation also illustrated how an old repo man never loses the eyes and the nose for goods gone astray.

I was working for a steel company as credit manager. Sales were down sharply. I had just completed a free-lance consulting job for a medium-sized manufacturer on the East Coast, and had returned to my office to review new accounts that had been opened in my absence. One new account in particular caught my eye.

Here was a company that had been in business only for several months, but whose credit file indicated it was on the verge of becoming the next United States Steel. Our sales department said this new firm was buying and selling steel from every possible source, including most of our competitors. The company's principal, in his early 30s, reportedly had learned his trade well while working for other steel companies. Now, he appeared to have stumbled onto the trail to the end of the rainbow. At least, there seemed to be a pot of gold somewhere in his vicinity.

Our sales department, seeking to bring home its share of the gold, initiated a running gun battle with my credit department. The young man's new company had offered glowing references from other steel companies that recently had extended credit and had been paid promptly. To me, a company growing that fast—and ordering steel shipments as if they were sacks of potatoes—bore especially close scrutiny, no matter what the initial credit experience might have been. Several agonized months followed, in which management refereed the battle between my department and sales—which felt that its style was being cramped by our strict credit policies.

Ultimately, the young man's credit line was allowed to grow far beyond a wise limit. Hundreds of thousands of dollars worth of steel were delivered. It was all current within the more liberal credit terms when the sales department stopped receiving orders.

Several phone calls to our still-new customer went unanswered. Normally, it would not yet be time for the credit department to begin collection activities, because the account was current. Nevertheless, I was concerned.

Members of our management, sales and credit staff all had visited our new customer as we courted and serviced his account. I nevertheless decided to make my own unannounced, non-courting visit to the customer's place of business, in a medium-sized Tennessee city.

When I arrived, the office seemed normal; but the owner was not there. He was out of town, I was told, and would not be available for several days. Meanwhile, a quick look around revealed few signs of movement in the plant and warehouse. Plenty of inventory was on hand, and I suspected most of it to be a result of credit extensions by my firm and our competitors.

I decided to do a little sleuthing. I found out where the principal lived. That afternoon, I saw him coming to and from his home three or four times between 3 p.m. and 6 p.m. When he left at 6, I also left and got some dinner. Then, instead of going back to his house, I decided to see what was going on at the plant and warehouse.

When I arrived, about 9:30, the drowsy daytime scene had been replaced by one of the greatest displays of activity I had ever seen. About eight trucks were being loaded, and at least half of the inventory appeared headed out the door. The owner was not only in town, but he was obviously in total command of this bustling nocturnal movement of inventory. He was not only shocked but also confused when I pulled in the parking lot and announced my arrival.

What do you say when confronted with a situation that obviously is suspect? It's not so much what you say as how you say it. The trucks were taking deliveries to customers, the principal said, speaking in feverish terms as if he were warning of an impending tornado.

I told him I was notifying the local FBI office and that I was immediately retaining an attorney to seek an injunction to stop removal of the inventory to wherever it was going. Realizing he had been caught red-handed, the young principal admitted that neither he nor his company had any funds. He agreed to let me remove the portion of inventory that had been purchased from my firm, but not yet paid for. Within 24 hours, I arranged to have trucks haul the steel back to Detroit. A serious potential loss was averted by the good, gray McTevia, who—on the job at least—was living squarely in the present.

You'll note that it takes two to do the Living in the Future tango, whether or not greed extends to fraud. One party asks for the chips to live in the future; somebody else passes them through the window. The young steel man built a pyramid scheme of credit, but he didn't break into an office in the dead of night to get it. Somebody gave it to him—*fought* for permission to give it to him. The same applies to a local hardware purveyor who eagerly sends a mortgaged lawn mower out the door, or a multimillion-dollar savings and loan that eagerly sends its depositors' cash out the door to build a resort in the desert. In the extreme, it becomes a fine line between extending credit and aiding and abetting.

How many times have you read a newspaper story about the latest pigeon drop, or watched an earnest local TV consumer reporter warn viewers to beware of strangers at the door promising to turn a $50 bill into $500? How many times have you said to yourself: "Anybody who falls for that is really feeble, really dumb, really gullible, or really greedy"? So it goes in the business world, where you will find few feeble, dumb or gullible people. It seems, however, there is always someone eager to turn a buck, and willing to offer a customer transport to a destination far into the future.

As a federal bankruptcy trustee I have come upon numerous disaster scenes where Living in the Future has extended into fraud, either intentionally and from the outset, or out of the desperation that follows failure to meet a financial problem head-on. The creditor's nightmare—a sinking ship from which the captain is tossing anything salvageable to his friends and heirs—does occur, and far too often. It is no wonder, and totally forgivable, that the faces I encounter at creditors' meetings are not generally filled with trust and forgiveness. Preferences—

paying obligations to preferred creditors or relatives while ig-noring others—is the most common deceit indulged in by troub-led companies.

In one incredibly jumbled bankruptcy case in which I was appointed trustee, a major Detroit-area supermarket chain re-vealed itself to be cannibalized by what might be called *self-*preferences. In other words, the principal was draining cash from the company by, among other numerous methods, over-billing for products delivered from other companies he owned or controlled. These bills were paid, while other suppliers to the troubled chain were left holding the bag. The markets, and their employees, were beyond saving by the time I became involved in the case.

When greed and access to cash collide, sometimes the re-sulting behavior becomes as uncontrollable as a serial killer who will continue doing his evil thing—amid a maelstrom of investigation and publicity—until caught in the act. In one re-markable such instance, I was acting as trustee in a major bank-ruptcy case and had been sorting out the damage for a year and a half when I discovered a fraud riding piggyback on a Living in the Future disaster. A financial officer in the troubled organi-zation had found a way to divert revenues into his own pockets. Even as I worked closely with him to help the organization stem its negative cash flow, he continued to raid the till!

In essence, the nature of the operation was such that it received substantial payments in cash. The financial officer would pocket some of the money, then doctor the records. Only after meeting with some allegedly delinquent customers was I able to realize the discrepancy in the books and records. It seemed incredible to me that this would be going on not only before my arrival on the scene for a Chapter 11 reorganization, but afterward while I and my associates worked on the premises.

I informed the guilty party that we would be turning our information over to appropriate authorities. I told you that I have seen six people take their lives as a result of Living in the Future, and that five of them were principals of troubled compa-nies who could not live with the embarrassment of financial failure. This was the sixth. He shot himself to death the evening he was found out—as he must have known he inevitably would be.

The popular press and Hollywood sometimes would have you believe that the underworld—"organized crime"—has infiltrated half of the small- to medium-sized companies in the country, accounting for the demise of many. To the best of my knowledge, I have been involved in only one case where somebody very organized and very criminal was laundering cash. That is the classic mob use of a small company, and in this instance it was being used in a big way.

It was one of my very first cases as a receiver under the old Bankruptcy Act. Apparently, the owners of the corporation were involved in a serious dispute. One wanted to file for protection under Chapter 11; one didn't. But a petition was filed, and I was appointed. The company had stopped operating, and was out of cash.

I immediately went to the company's premises, sent the remainder of the employees home, changed the locks, seized the financial records and checkbooks, and began analyzing the company's operations and assets to determine whether it should continue in business.

I acted so swiftly that I apparently got my hands on more extensive records than anyone had anticipated. It didn't take me long to figure out that I was in the middle of my very first fraud audit. The company's annual sales were $3,000,000, but hundreds of thousands were being passed through the company *every week*. By the time I had analyzed cash flow, it was clear that some $15,000,000 had passed through this $3,000,000 company in one year.

Within two weeks of my appointment, and with my analysis in only the preliminary stage, the owners filed a motion in court to dismiss the Chapter 11 proceedings. All Chapter 11 costs were paid, all unsecured creditors were paid, and I was ordered to return the books and records to the debtors—which I promptly did. Within 24 hours, the person to whom I had been instructed to return the books and records (which I later learned disappeared mysteriously) was involved in a very unusual and fatal automobile accident.

TV and the movies to the contrary, of all the dark activity and outright fraud I have encountered, only the little company with the huge cash flow showed any signs of having accepted an offer it couldn't refuse.

Fascinating as it may be, I admit that this talk of fraud and criminal activity seems somehow a digression from our theme, as if we have moved from talking about household disputes to talking about someone gone berserk with an Uzi in the town square. I don't mean to suggest that young Bill Dunn ought to do hard time for falling behind in his bills, or that a company with a serious payables problem is somehow the same as a fraud-riddled grocery chain. There *is* a linkage, however, a progression along which a crucial point finally is crossed and the red lights start blinking and whirling. The Living in the Future practitioner no longer is merely tampering with ethics and sound finance; he is skirting, and then flouting, the law.

Some who argue that there is such a thing as a "victimless" crime cite prostitution as an example. But when a company or institution begins prostituting itself to cope with Living in the Future, there are victims galore. And the company, and its principals, wind up only inches from the red-light tip of that progression toward felonious behavior. Instead of bullet-riddled bodies lying on the town square, mortally wounded columns of numbers are strewn about. Hundreds, thousands—millions—of people may be seriously injured, but it just doesn't have the drama and the impact of a berserk gunman.

It would take battalions of well-armed crazies a month of unresisted rampage to inflict as much damage on the populace as that unleashed by the savings and loan debacle. The average citizen, however, can recite more details about a sensational homicide a thousand miles away than he can about a financial disaster so huge that it impacts our society's ability to repair a crumbling bridge a block down the street. Amazing.

Ethics, morality, *legality* must be applied to columns of numbers as surely as they must be applied to citizens walking the streets. As a people, we must learn to see the destructive behavior pattern that extends from personal Living in the Future all the way to the national debt. I think most of us, in an era when crime is a pre-eminent fear of so many, can understand the behavior pattern that extends from children who do not learn respect for property—or even life—to adults who rob, maim and kill. That is why I am not the least bit afraid, no matter what the academics may think of it, to write an anecdotal book in which I talk in the same breath of childhood allowances and corporate finance, of Blonde Goddesses and government spending run amok, of auto loans gone bad and leveraged desert spas repossessed.

Was that young steel entrepreneur "just doing some crafty business?" No. He was a crook, as sure as a young man snatching an old woman's purse on the sidewalk is a crook. Such connections have to be made in the public consciousness before these grave problems can be addressed. It starts with our own personal approach to the financial marathon, and builds from there. Because in a nation of shoplifters, the bank robber would be king.

27

The Ultimate Living in the Future Scheme

I expected a modest turnout, but the auditorium was full. I expected to talk for half an hour, but I talked for half a day.

The audience was there not to hear one of my lectures, but out of mortal fear. Each of the several hundred persons in the room saw his or her life—not the materialistic trappings of "the good life," but the basic requirements of life itself—slipping away along with an ill-conceived plan based on Living in the Future.

It was deep tragedy with a slapstick facade, and it launched one of the most emotional business engagements of my life. From that point forward I became not just a consultant with an eye for the human side of these situations, but one with a deepened awareness that troubled balance sheets are not even the tip of the iceberg. Better to think of them as the radar blip alerting you that something menacing is out there in the real world. Only after you emerge from the radar room and eyeball the situation do you have a genuine notion of what an iceberg looks like.

The meeting took so long because every person in the auditorium was a senior citizen. Half the people could not hear me, and the other half had a very difficult time understanding what I was trying to explain. Every time I repeated what I had to say, another individual—finally hearing or finally comprehending the message—would offer a response. All this in what once had been the grand ballroom of a once-grand hotel along the Detroit River. That was the slapstick facade.

The tragedy lay in the reality what these old people were saying and what they were fearing. Many spoke with tears in their eyes, all of them with a sense of betrayal and hopelessness in their hearts. They were speaking to me as a bankruptcy receiver. If I could not keep the situation under control, keep the food suppliers paid, keep the utilities paid, keep the medical personnel paid, then these senior citizens were in grave danger of being put out on the curb like so much liquidated inventory.

This was my first encounter with one of the most shaky, and certainly the most symbolic, of all Living in the Future schemes: the life care concept. Each of these old folks had put up a substantial amount of cash—$25,000 to $70,000—which, along with a monthly fee, was supposed to provide them with an apartment in the recycled hotel, meals and a certain amount of care until the day they died. Before I arrived on the ballroom stage, in its heyday the scene of many gala upper-crust social gatherings, every person in my audience had read in the local newspapers that the "life care" facility was in trouble and might be shut down.

Eventually I would deal with 10 bankruptcies or restructurings of retirement centers. All had religious affiliations, and all promised the same amenities to their residents for the rest of their lives on Earth. These cases were part of a nationwide flood of unrealistic geriatric leveraging. At one point, when one of the largest such operations was collapsing in the Pacific Northwest, *Sixty Minutes* interviewed me about the phenomenon.

The churches, the actuaries, the leveragers and the medical establishment—each concerned with the future but in far different ways—collided in a twisted heap of belief, demographic projections, unrealistic debt and scientific progress. Sitting in the middle of this intersection, broadsided and battered, were legions of old people who thought they had been guaranteed something every old person yearns for: security. Instead, they were consumed by chaos and uncertainty.

The business plan for all these centers was simple, if grievously flawed. The resident would purchase a contract, often by surrendering most of his or her net worth. Then, much as a restaurant manager thinks not in terms of tossing a salad but of turning over table occupancy, management would sell and re-sell each residence unit as its occupants died. There would be not only perpetual care, but perpetual profit.

The corporation that operated the riverfront facility, among others, was the very first of these corporations where I was summoned to serve as bankruptcy receiver or trustee. I soon determined that whoever had prepared the actuarial study upon which the business plan was based must have been out of his mind. Either that, or he lived in blissful ignorance of the obvious fact that modern medicine was daily extending life expectancy, turning actuarial tables to confetti. This same flaw would prevail in every such case with which I dealt.

Put yourself in the shoes of the retirees I met in that ballroom. There they sat, facing the prospect of losing lodgings they were expecting to call home for the rest of their lives. They already had spent all their money to pay the bill. Their only transgression was that they *had lived too long.* After spending a lifetime facing their own financial difficulties, they had in good faith fulfilled their end of a bargain only to discover that their daily breath represented, in essence, a receivable gone bad by being good. Management couldn't pay its bills because the tables weren't being turned over fast enough. The old folks were lingering too long over life's plate!

For the first time, I realized completely just how impossible it is for old people to live the new American Way—solving financial problems by dipping into the future. There is not much leverage in a Social Security check. Ultimately, considering the alternative, we all hope to grow old. What will happen when the most leveraged generation reaches 65 or 70, I don't even care to contemplate. But for the old people in the auditorium, who had passed through their productive years before Living in the Future became the norm, none of what was happening to them made the least bit of sense. They had always paid their bills, usually up front, and now they were discovering that they had purchased not a home for the rest of their lives but rather a unit in a highly leveraged and troubled investment scheme.

Over the two years that I helped reorganize this particular retirement center—actually a group of retirement homes and health-care facilities—a number of residents died. Many of these deaths obviously were not actuarially correct. But I often wonder how many were hastened by the turmoil and uncertainty caused by management's financial imprudence. I am sure that at least some of these deaths resulted from a morbid sense that there was nowhere else to go. It was the only future they could foresee, and they entered it.

Every case is an education for me, in one respect or another. This one—and the retirement center cases that followed—were the equivalent of a graduate degree. Tell me, where does my usual message fit with senior citizens? How do I say, "This company may die, but you will not"? There is no discussion of starting over, of retreating into the present and living within your financial reality. For these old people, the buck already has stopped squarely in their laps.

Maybe those of us in our 30s, 40s and even 50s are deluding ourselves when we talk knowingly of how teenagers believe they are immortal and, therefore, do such wild and crazy things. Maybe the lesson of mortality, and of a finite approach to everything from finances to public policy, is not really learned until it will not require a drunk driver or a carcinoma, but merely a new page on the calendar, to bring us to the end of our line.

At any rate, I learned something from looking into the eyes of these desperate and frightened elderly people. Sometimes I saw my parents. Sometimes I saw my 94-year-old grandmother. Mostly I saw living proof of what I knew and preached in the abstract: that this insane leveraged lifestyle our society has adopted cannot be rolled over and over with each passing day. No matter how skillful the player, the game has to end somewhere. These retirement centers were one such place, where you could not avert your eyes and where you could not say, "Tomorrow will be another day."

I work hard for every hour that I bill, but I've never worked harder than I did on these cases. Technically speaking, these senior citizens were not clients so much as they were my bankrupt clients' slow-moving inventory. But it was the elderly for whom I worked. I did not want to see one of them turned out on the street.

Turning around a retirement home or a hospital—another kind of institution I have successfully reorganized—is an entirely different kind of challenge. When you lay off employees to gain economies, you are often endangering lives. You cannot say, "Revenues do not match costs, so we're going to send the night shift home."

It was a series of incredible tasks, but—eventually, with a lot of agony for all concerned—we got each of the jobs done. Actuarial realities instead of pipe dreams became the basis for budgets. The homes were transferred to a pay-as-you-go basis for new residents, who were recruited despite obvious fears resulting from publicity of the financial crises. No one was turned out onto the street.

I am myself a churchgoer, and most certainly do not wish to sound anti-Christian in any way. But there was an obvious lesson to be learned here about religion-sponsored businesses, and a further revelation of just how great an enticement Living in the Future can be.

Not all religiously run institutions operate on the same principles, of course. But I saw church and financial interests meet, under the aegis of long-established and legitimate denominations, in shocking ways. Retirement home corporations garbed themselves in the trappings of religion, portraying not only the hereafter but the future as their province, and sold their product with the zeal of a preacher. In many cases, each congregation which sent a new resident received a cash bonus. There were, in effect, sales commissions. If a used-car salesman can profit from a nickname like "Honest John," you can only imagine the goodwill a salesman can bring to a closing if he is perceived somehow as a representative of the prospect's church.

If a church wishes to sponsor a business, it would seem to me that the church ought to impose some very tight controls on the sales organization—particularly when lives are at stake. Faith is a wonderful thing. But when books must be balanced lest someone die of neglect, it is not a viable business plan simply to trust that God will provide.

That's the obvious lesson.

The revelation was really more of a surmise.

If a church—our strongest symbol of resistance to materialism—can be drawn into a scheme such as this, how in the world can anyone be expected to resist Living in the Future? Maybe you need plastic to get past those Pearly Gates.

Or maybe what really happened in Eden was that God, being angry with Adam and Eve, punished them by changing the terms for acquiring all the marvelous fruits of the garden: Henceforth, Adam and Eve could take what they wanted, but only on the installment plan.

No wonder they looked at each other and were ashamed.

PART FOUR

A Society in Trouble

28

Admitting We Have a Problem

A couple of years ago I watched a TV documentary about lemmings. It was uncanny to see a cliched figure of speech—"like lemmings to the sea"—come to life on the screen. The poor little creatures scurried frantically toward certain death, eager to get there, pouring over the cliff, first the leaders and then the followers sailing energetically into the abyss.

With the TV clicked off and my head on my pillow, I couldn't erase the image. I thought of all the clients I've dealt with. I thought of our society Living in the Future, with people—rather than these doomed little creatures—eagerly pressing themselves to and over the edge. At the bottom of the cliff, in my drowsy but insistent imaging, lay a tangled pile of bills and bankruptcy papers awaiting disposal by the next generation.

I've thought of that documentary many times. And I can't help but dwell on a basic difference between the lemmings I watched on TV and the Americans I have watched, in an increasing horde, throwing themselves over the financial cliff. Lemmings, so far as anyone knows, have *always* surged toward a senseless death. The lemming's death wish is innate. Americans, however, have learned the trick within my lifetime.

Occasionally a small-town newspaper will still print a story about a celebratory mortgage-burning. Usually it's a church congregation lighting the happy flame, churches being one of the last institutions to shed old values. I can remember when a married couple would make double or triple payments and then toss the *home* mortgage in the fireplace as a declaration of independence. Now, only in my mid-50s, I live in a society where almost any viable automobile is mortgaged, to say nothing of most gourmet meals and a good percentage of TV sets and home appliances.

Sometime in the last 35 years, America parted company with a fundamental concept that allows a society to function with stability from one generation to the next. We began to ignore the relationship between *having* something and *paying* for it. This assures eventual economic chaos, but the fallout extends far beyond narrow matters of commerce and finance. Our society has lost a good many things besides a paid-up account at the general store.

As a people, we have crassly translated our old values, including all those noble words about freedom, into a phrase that to my knowledge you will find nowhere in the writings of Jefferson, Adams, Hamilton or any of the other founding fathers. It's a phrase that in recent decades has become the new code for signaling our society's greatest point of pride, the thing we treasure most among all the attributes that separate our society from the rest of the world. It has nothing to do with triumph over tyranny. It has nothing to do with the Bill of Rights. It is a truly ugly phrase, when you think about it: *the American standard of living*.

It is ugly because it is a standard that has come to speak of nothing but materialism. Not of freedom, not of the right to pursue the life path of our choice, not of the right to worship at any altar we wish, not of a justice system that quickly and fairly deals with criminals, not of anything envisioned by the signers of the Constitution. Instead, our *standard* of living measures only how many consumer goods we can accumulate in our living rooms and in our garages. That, we have come to believe, is what makes America special.

It's a long journey from "give me liberty or give me death"

to "give me a split-level and a new car with a cellular phone—at all costs." But we have gotten there.

As a national ideal it is both morally and economically bankrupt. It is not much different from the undisciplined child wailing in a toy store because no one has taught him that he can't have it all. Like that child, Americans—individually and collectively—have become willing to utter any unkeepable promise just so we can walk away with all the toys we can carry. Clinging to the myth that every succeeding generation can live amid greater materialistic comforts, we have been willing to take on the wildest, most unrealistic obligations—assuming that every dawn will be brighter than the one before.

In order to reap these unrealistic rewards, to lay claim to this precious ever-escalating materialistic standard of living, individuals began living far into the future. Corporations began living far into the future. And our federal government—at the most recent count, if you can consider such an inconceivable number to be countable—ran up a $4 trillion debt. This is not a *loan,* this is not finance; this is, quite simply, spending money that belongs to citizens yet unborn. In the real financial world, any party to such a rape of trust would be indicted and—even if the prosecutor were drunk or incompetent—convicted of a felony.

At the apparent end of a Cold War which for 45 years kept us peering outward in search of enemies, the cold truth turns out to be just as Pogo said years ago: "We have met the enemy, and he is us." We have clamped the shackles of unrealistic debt, at a level never approached in world history, upon ourselves. Freedom has been taken hostage, without a shot being fired.

When my life and career experiences first alerted me to what Living in the Future was doing to our nation, any attempt at discourse on the subject was liable to be viewed as "political," or "a matter of philosophy." It was as if choosing between unrealistic debt and solvency were a question of taste, like choosing between paisley or solid neckties. Living in the Future was seen as a sort of esthetics, a new lifestyle, rather than a redefinition of reality, something with hard and real consequences. Simply put, nobody wanted to talk about it.

Now the bills are coming due. The national debt and a profusion of unrealistic public obligations are about to become the issue of the decade. Painful and agonizing decisions will have to be made. Failure to make them will lead to an unprecedented crisis in our legislatures and on our streets. This is not political analysis. This is just an old credit man commenting on a situation that for years has been as obvious as the numbers on the balance sheet of a company spinning toward self-destruction.

I do not need to tell you that today's kids may be the first American generation to live *less well* than their parents. Stiller and Meara, the comedy team, sum it up in the moving-van radio commercial that is contemporary to this manuscript. The van is on the way, she says, to move things onto the sunporch—because the kids are coming home to live. What about the so-and-so's, he asks plaintively. *Their* kids just returned home. Are the so-and-so's living on their sunporch? No, she says, they've moved into the garage.

On the sunporch, in the garage—"in the basement" is the figurative phrase I like to use for this sad phenomenon—and, we should add, jointly buried in a $4 trillion national debt incurred by their forebears. With questionable prospects for the revenue side of their ledger, our young people must start life's marathon bearing the burden of $4 trillion in obligations they never asked for. Slowly but surely, they are coming to understand what has been done to them and to their children, and the fact that the burden is growing by the day.

Meanwhile, Americans who do have new cars with cellular phones meet reality face to face at the top of almost any urban freeway exit ramp. Homeless, jobless, hopeless souls wander our streets in vast and growing numbers. They are merely the most visible members of our unleveraged class. The gap between the haves (who acquired much of their "standard of living" by leveraging it) and the have-nots (who possess not an ounce of leveraging power) also is growing by the day.

Is it any wonder that the have-nots—homeless or otherwise —do not feel they are even a part of our society? Modern reckoning does not count the non-materialistic things we *all* have, or used to have, as Americans. Shared ideals and a sense that life goes on without a profusion of toys are not a component of our new standard of living. That may be the greatest difference between a have-not of the early '90s and a have-not of the Great Depression. The legions of Americans who struggled through those lean years did not live in a culture that insisted, "You are *supposed* to have things, you are *entitled* to have things." Today, ubiquitous TV commercials—the one thing that *is* shared by every citizen—declare there is not only a chicken in every pot, but a touring sedan in every garage.

We are well into evolution as a tribe split into two camps. Dwellers in one camp have no material possessions of consequence, no plastic, no condo. They have no job, or a job that cannot begin to sustain a family. The jobless ones possess only large amounts of time, in which they may ponder their exclusion from the advertised norm. Dwellers in the other camp possess all manner of highly leveraged toys and a relatively safe and comfortable address—but have no time whatsoever. They scurry like lemmings to service their debt, seldom even sitting down to eat dinner as a family. One would have to be incredibly naive to doubt for a moment which camp is the more desirable place to be. But, to my observation, precious few dwellers in either camp are happy.

As the gap between the two camps widens, we inch ever nearer to becoming a police state. Huge expenditures are made on prisons, but there is room for few but the most hardened criminals. When we are obsessed with having things at all costs, when we *define* ourselves by what we have, people do go out and get them. Some do so by Living in the Future. Some do so by holding up a liquor store. The thief or a murderer is no less guilty, no less reprehensible, no less deserving of punishment. I am merely noting that the replacement of moral and idealistic standards by a phony materialism—and the rampant growth of a phony Daddy Warbucks vision of public policy based on Living in the Future—incubate crime.

A good case, in fact, can be made that Living in the Future

itself should be a crime under law. When a man says, "I want something, so I'm going to take a gun and rob a store," our society says that is a felony. We don't care how badly he wants the money—or even how badly he may *need* the money—we put him in jail, if there is room.

But what is the difference between the holdup man and a government that steals from unborn generations to satisfy current perceived needs? Forget what the expenditures may be; it is irrelevant. I personally, for example, do not want thousands of my tax dollars spent to measure rainfall in the Mojave Desert. But whether I approve or disapprove is irrelevant to our discussion. Some Americans do not want a penny of their tax dollars spent to build warplanes. That is irrelevant to our discussion. Some Americans believe society *needs* greater government expenditures on health care, or elderly care, or highways, or any number of problems the worthiness of which is difficult to deny. But that is *all irrelevant* to our discussion.

What *is* relevant is a return to a fundamental truth of life: that to have something, worthy or otherwise, you must pay for it. It may *seem* that things—including noble public programs— can be acquired or implemented without paying, by setting the bill aside on the desk to be taken care of another day. But by now I hope I have shared enough of my experiences to convince you that only chaos lies down that path. People or companies or societies that bury themselves in debt gradually and totally lose—to put it strictly in pragmatic terms—their flexibility. They become strangled by unrealistic obligations, unable to cope with even minor crises. They begin to prostitute themselves. Then, financially, they *die*.

Even Mother Theresa, as far as I know, works on a cash basis. Otherwise there would not be a single suffering person left in Calcutta.

If you follow even the TV news out of Washington, you know that the current buzzword in any discussion of our federal budget is "entitlements." The congressman's face appears on TV, and he says something like: "Gee, we'd like to trim spending, but we're locked in to so many *entitlement* programs. There's

really just a tiny percentage of the budget that we can touch."
Inflexibility. Strangulation. Unrealistic obligations. Living in
the Future.

The great strength of our government is that it reflects the
character of its people. That is, of course, a two-edged sword. Is
it any wonder that a nation Living in the Future elects a Congress that runs the credit meter beyond measurement, then—as
a footnote—kites its own personal checks? Is it any wonder that,
just as Bill Dunn found himself working for nothing but a futile
pass at clearing his monthly bills, you and I now must work five
months a year just to pay our taxes? Is it any wonder that a
significant amount of that tax bill goes for nothing but interest
on a debt run up because government provides services without
paying for them? The people we have sent to Washington are,
like most of our society, accustomed to Living in the Future. In
Washington they have found the largest lever in the universe,
and they have pulled it.

Individuals can leverage themselves from here to Tulsa.
But inevitably, if a person somehow manages to sustain a serious financial problem for decades, he at least will "solve" it by
dying.

Companies can leverage themselves from here to Tokyo.
That is a long way, but it is a finite distance. Companies that
live too far into the future invariably do one of two things: they
reel themselves back to the present, or they die.

Our federal government, alas, can leverage itself—*has leveraged itself*—not from here to the moon but to Jupiter or Ura-
nus, someplace so far that only certain Ph.D's can measure the
distance. There is no provision in the Constitution for any three
creditors to force Congress into involuntary bankruptcy, to bring
the scam to a halt. That is probably because none of the 18th
Century gentlemen who wrote our Constitution could even con-
ceive of Living in the Future. In fact, this superhuman, super-
corporate ability of the government to leverage its leverage,
year after year, has been conceived and implemented only
within the lifetime of anyone reading this book.

The resulting monster resembles a slithering Hollywood

special-effects creature. It can be hacked at or blowtorched or strafed by puny fighter planes, but it just leverages itself once again and keeps growing. It sustains its humongous body by sucking oxygen and nutrients that rightfully belong to Americans who are not yet born. Unlike you or me, or a troubled company, government—it would appear—can carry off the scam indefinitely because it does not die.

I am not so sure. If the federal government does not succeed in borrowing itself to death, the people may yet rise up and smother it through strength of numbers. It could be the haves, or it could be the have-nots, who finally do the creature in. The citizens standing on either side of the deepening have/have-not chasm have their reasons. The Daddy Warbucks mentality has not, as study after study assures us, done much of a job toward bringing the have-nots into "the American standard of living." The haves, meanwhile, are likely to assume a revolutionary bent as Tax Freedom Day moves past June 1 and on toward Dec. 31. An alternative scenario, of course, would require the government to survive because troops will be necessary to keep the haves and have-nots from each other's throats. We already have a taste of that sad, frightening, devastating scenario.

I am not, however, in the business of filling in the blanks and making specific predictions about our society and our government. And I am not an economist, so I cannot construct any model with hydrologic imagery like "trickle down" on the one hand or "pump priming" on the other in an effort to explain what is going on. But it is perfectly clear to me that the greatest society of the 20th Century lies in mortal danger of chaos and disintegration because of *debt*. Our personal and collective willingness to spend money we don't have—first in amounts that it is uncertain we ever will have, then in amounts that we *know* we never will have—lies at the root of our great anxiety, current pain and future agony.

The dynamic is the same, as I've tried to illustrate, in every professional case I have encountered—from "Bill Dunn" to large corporations. So much so that sometimes the repetition of circumstance and behavior, and my ability to foresee from experience exactly how the script will play out, makes what I do for a living seem incredibly simple. I cannot tell you how painful it is to have watched for more than a decade as our once-proud nation—teeming with scholars and businessmen and even politicians far wiser than I—has slid into *precisely* the same situation that I deal with every day. I shouldn't have to remind you that most of the entities that I deal with are at the brink, and that a very large percentage of them cannot be saved.

Unlike a few years ago, however, one begins to hear serious talk of debt as a real problem instead of as a way of life. It remains true that a political candidate of either party who brings a message of realism to the voters soon becomes a former candidate. But there is talk, and there will be more talk. And one day, one hopes, there will be action. As in any serious financial crisis, it becomes a question of meeting the problem head-on—and soon enough to do some good.

This being a democracy, it must begin with the people. The problem began with the people, and it must begin to end with the people. There are small signs of that occurring. Significant amounts of personal debt have been paid down in the most recent recession. Interest rates hit bottom, but without a rush on the markets—except to refinance existing debt at lower rates. Partly that is because so many people could not possibly live one inch farther into the future. But partly it is because more people are becoming uneasy with unrealistic debt. Ironically, many of the gurus cheerleading for recovery would have us rushing out to run our plastic up into the stratosphere once again. That is not recovery. That is easing the pain of alcoholism by swallowing a fifth of bourbon. Perhaps as a people we are smarter than that.

Perhaps, with utter disaster staring us in the face, we are about to take that first step and say, all together, "We have a problem."

I told you that sometimes businessmen trapped by Living in the Future go into their offices, pull the blinds and never come out. In a way, we—and our leaders—have done just that. We have gotten ourselves into the most serious financial problem conceivable, one involving trillions of dollars and every citizen of the most powerful nation on Earth. Personal and corporate bankruptcies have soared to record levels. The United States government itself is—by any practical definition of the term—bankrupt. A few people, however, are peeking out from behind the blinds, summoning the courage to come out on the shop floor and address the problem.

No, I don't think there will be a shortage of discussion about these issues in the months and years ahead, and that is a welcome ray of sunshine on this dim tableau.

Consider, however, the impediments to solving a serious financial crisis involving, say, a small tool-and-die company: Denial of the problem by the principals, competing claims from creditors, a lack of economic flexibility to deal with the problem, the absolute need to act *now.* Multiply all these impediments by however many zeroes it takes to maneuver in trillions, by however many interest groups have laid claim to a slice of the federal budget, by whatever denial and intransigence lie in the heart of a politician who has made a living portraying Daddy Warbucks, by the amount of time it takes a bureaucracy to do *anything.* Reversing that tide is an overwhelming prospect, even for a turnaround specialist.

Here is why it can be done: because solutions to problems of great magnitude and complexity require an equally imposing impetus for change. Is revolution a sufficiently imposing impetus for change? We'll find out, because revolution is the direction in which we are headed unless our society begins to live within its means, and thereby rediscovers that its means are not its end.

The angry homeless and the angry affluent must return, together, to the present to iron things out.

29

The Biggest Restructuring
of Them All

Our society's values have become so crass, or foggy, or non-existent that the American mosaic lies in grave danger of coming totally unglued. Pieces of the grand design already hang precariously.

We are many tribes—defined by culture, ethnicity, belief, economic standing, vocation, geography—each with its own agenda. Further, I have my agenda and you have yours. Sometime, over a cup of coffee, it might be interesting to sit down and discuss the relative merits of our separate agendas. That is not what this book is about. It is about a *shared* agenda, or what should be a shared agenda. We are talking about survival, about whether there will be any viable arena in which you and I may agree to disagree, about whether a nation that persists in calling itself the greatest on Earth will continue to wither until it is reduced to nothing but a bankruptcy trustee and an answering service.

We are not there yet, but we are getting close. Our predominant manufactured product is hamburgers. The haves have been so busy leveraging that (aside from paying taxes) their main contribution has been to move money and consume material goods—which increasingly are manufactured offshore, leaving us an economy with the texture of white bread rather than steel. The have-nots have been so busy pressing for entitlements and developing an agenda portraying themselves purely as victims that they look beyond themselves for solutions, which is exactly the worst place to look. Both parties seem able to respond to no call except the dinner bell, pursuing their slice of some mythical self-perpetuating American pie. The range of moral, social, political and business issues arising from that scenario is so huge as to defy simple analysis or solution.

There is a simple starting point, however, and that is our government's stifling financial crisis and astronomical debt—its insistence on Living in the Future today, thereby imperiling the real future of the very nation it purports to serve.

As in the case of a single individual, our collective balance sheet reveals much about where we have gone astray. Our largest employer and largest spender is wildly out of control. Feeding on and mirroring our own personally bankrupt lifestyles, it is strangling our today and smothering our tomorrow. Restoring the breath of freedom and implementing a healthy lifestyle represents, or should represent, our shared agenda.

Bill Dunn, meet Uncle Sam.

Our society cannot be restructured until our government is restructured. Our government must be reeled back within its means, out of the future and into the present. Ours is still an affluent nation. But it will not remain so if a growing segment of the population looks to Washington for crumbs (and in some cases, steak), while citizens on the other side of the chasm find themselves working *most* of their hours in a futile attempt to prop up a bankrupt government. It should be obvious that chaos and revolution lie around the bend. Washington Inc. needs an out-of-court reorganization, and needs it now.

The simple, if painful, principles of that process should be applied to our government in exactly the same manner you have seen in the first three sections of this book.

It begins with admitting the problem.

I said in the previous chapter that Americans are beginning

to recognize and admit that Washington has a serious financial problem. On the face of it, that seems ridiculous. *Of course* Washington has a serious financial problem. But denial and Living in the Future are a powerful tandem. Bill Dunn shuffled that stack of overdue notices for a long time before he realized what an unrealistic world he had created, that financially he was somewhere on Mars, that it was impacting his life in ways far beyond some numbers in his checkbook. In the corporate world, MBA's in charge of companies teetering on the brink can look you straight in the eye and sum up their situation by saying: "We have a little cash-flow problem." In Washington, denial achieves ultra-sophisticated heights where reality disappears without a trace. A little short on cash? Call in the leveragers and write them a T-bill. Problem? What problem?

When the federal government can routinely sign up for programs that amount to $10, $20 or *hundreds* of dollars for every man, woman and child in the United States without even a sense that money is being spent, we are talking about one of the most incredible unchecked abuses of power in the history of the world. Granted, something that costs *thousands* of dollars for every man, woman and child in the country—such as bailing out the S&L leveragers—does create a bit of a stir. But even the S&L debacle illustrates the amazing point. Imagine your unmitigated outrage if a stranger came to you door and informed you, "Excuse me, but I just took a couple thousand dollars out of your checking account to pay for a screwup that you had nothing to do with. Thank you." The money *is* coming out of your checking account. Without a trace. The only difference is, nobody said thanks.

So, although admitting Washington's serious financial problem wouldn't seem to be such a big step, it will be a *huge* step to move at last from lip service to full admission and understanding—to the brink of action. It will mean moving from la-la land into reality, from ignorance into awareness, from a sleepwalking state into consciousness.

Scott Peck wrote in *The Road Less Traveled:* "Political power is the capacity to coerce others, overtly or covertly, to do one's will. This capacity resides in a position, such as a kingship or a presidency, or else in money. It does not reside in the person who occupies the position or possesses the money. Consequently, political power is unrelated to goodness or wisdom. Very stupid and very evil people have walked as kings upon the Earth. Spiritual power, however, resides entirely within the individual and has nothing to do with the capacity to coerce others. People of great spiritual power may be wealthy and may on occasion occupy political positions of leadership, but they are as likely to be poor and lacking in political authority. Then, what is the capacity of spiritual power if not the capacity to coerce? It is the capacity to make decisions with maximum awareness. It is consciousness."

"Most people most of the time," Peck writes, *"make decisions with little awareness of what they are doing."* (My italics.)

That passage is the most eloquent explanation of Washington's fiscal *unconsciousness,* and the public's passive acceptance of Living in the Future, that I have encountered. There is, indeed, something more profound to this business than adding and subtracting numbers. It involves, simply put, understanding the consequences of Living in the Future. Placing this awareness in the context of a spiritual dimension goes a long way toward explaining my firm belief that our collective loss of values and our collective loss of financial consciousness are vitally linked.

So we must get on with step one, the business of consciousness-raising, of admitting our government's miserable and debilitating bankruptcy. I fervently hope that I am correct in my impression that such awareness is a growing thing. This book is one small attempt to help get us all to that shared agenda, to step one. When we get there, the next step will be—as you know—both simple and painful.

It will bruise some politicians' egos to learn that they are but an intermediary step. For, once the problem is admitted, it follows automatically that people with that spiritual dimension of awareness will sit in our national legislature. This can involve new faces, or it can involve old faces with new awareness. It matters little whose name tag is affixed to each overstuffed chair on the floor of Congress because—as Peck says—the power resides in the office and in the purse strings it controls, not in the particular representatives who sit on either side of the aisle. We can throw the current chair-sitters out of office, or we can raise their consciousness. Either way will do, because the will of the people still prevails in this country. The hard truth is that the will of a people desperately Living in the Future is exactly what has gotten us into, and kept us in, this desperate situation.

Step one, then, will get us to step two, whether or not our current representatives respond to a new public consciousness. And step two is where the intense pain must begin, along with the problem's solution. Our government must restructure its finances. It must take the Road Less Traveled.

Like Bill Dunn or General Motors, government has three options: It can increase revenues, it can decrease expenses, or it can do both.

In the case of government, facing up to those options is a uniquely tricky enterprise. When I consult with the principal of a troubled company, very rarely can he do anything that he has not already done to increase revenues—short of liquidating assets. There will be those in government, however, who will say: "By gosh, you're right. We have a problem. Let's increase revenues." And government, being the unique entity that it is, *can* send out for more money. It can take even more wealth from you and me. It can take even more wealth from our unborn grandchildren. It can—in the ultimate stage of government bankruptcy—pay its bills by *printing* more money. If a wheelbarrow of currency is needed to pay for a Big Mac, you will know that government has exercised its unique ability to settle for five cents on the dollar while meeting every obligation at face value.

Let me assure you that, from this vantage point, government will have one hellacious time increasing revenues—by any of those methods—without finally taking us over the brink. My own view is that Tax Freedom Day already falls so late in the year that it must be regarded as a major cause of our pale economy, of our lack of true productive investment that creates jobs, of our diminishing incentive to work hard and believe that there is a point to it all. I don't think I want to be around when Tax Freedom Day falls on December 31, when I will have to work all year so government can provide services that it cannot afford to provide.

But that is not the half of it. We taxpayers are increasingly paying the bill not for services rendered, but merely for service on our collective debt. We have been reduced, as a society, to the pathetic reflection of millions of hopelessly buried individuals scurrying like lemmings to make the minimum monthly payment on their various pieces of plastic. Reducing principal has become virtually out of our reach. We have consumed unrealistically. We juggle the bills, pay the interest, and cower in an anxiety-ridden state while our lawmakers decide what account to charge next.

It is time for government to do what people, and companies, do when they face up to this dismal situation. It is time to reduce expenses. To pay the bills down. To live within our means. To endure the pain. To emerge from the agony of it all with a sense of renewal, with new values, with an understanding that we can't have it all and that we have become desperately unhappy trying to do so. To be free.

No one has ever before created such a monstrous financial mess. Consequently, short of war, it is possible that what we must do as a people will be one of the most painful things we ever have done. The nation's largest employer will have to send people home by the scores of thousands. Some citizens with entitlements will find that they are entitled to less. Programs that lack no virtues save affordability will have to be chopped.

This acutely necessary restructuring will be the toughest test of American democratic processes in my lifetime. I tend to think that democracy can handle it. Given the alternative, we have no choice but to find out. We are in much the same position as a surgical patient who can select two options: (a) lose a limb or two, or (b) let the cancer spread. Our nation must assume the task of a financially buried family sitting down around the dining room table, its multitude of overdue bills spread around for all to see, deciding how to downsize its lifestyle and return to reality.

Sometime in the hopefully near future, to offer just one prediction, "prioritizing" will become one of the busiest words on the evening news. Because from somewhere in the vast smorgasbord of government spending, massive deletions must be made. The debate will be raucous. Cowards will abound. The heroes' recognition as such will come mainly from future generations. Inertia will be a potent force, which is why the process cannot begin until that first step is taken with a serious and clearly purposeful stride. Americans must truly "ask not what their country can do for them," with the enthusiasm not only of patriotic rhetoric but of enlightened self-interest.

That is the optimistic side of my gloomy message. It seems to me that restructuring *will* occur because it *must* occur if we are to survive. My great fear is that, as in most financial restructurings, it will occur too late.

It is not my purpose here to press my agenda over yours, or my clan's agenda over your clan's, or my region's agenda over your region's. The only agenda that I strongly wish to press is that we all gather around that table—soon—with a conviction that we will not leave until the hard decisions have been made. In an enterprise as huge, complex and multi-missioned as the United States government, an infinite number of restructuring plans are possible. The important element—just as with a troubled company that must sell its plan to its creditors, and then successfully follow it through—is that the plan must be realistic. We are not talking about some vague "austerity plan" that reduces a few departmental budgets without making a dent in the core problem. We are talking about radical change, about positive cash flow, about *paying down the national debt.* That is the only realistic approach, and that is the only approach that the creditors' committee—you and I—should accept.

The democratic process will decide which agendas survive and which agendas die. Will most of the military go home, removing the United States from its role of world policeman? Are

government retirement and health-care benefits realistic, or do
we need to return to the privatized approach that prevailed into
the lifetimes of some people now receiving those benefits? Will
the government continue to finance space exploration, or will
that activity be set aside for some generation that can afford it?
Will the government—which owns, for example, massive tracts
of land dedicated to bombing practice—sell off some assets? Will
the government continue to finance broadcasting systems here
and abroad? Will the government continue to finance measurement of rainfall in the Mojave desert?

I don't know. But the decisions must be made, with the
same timeliness, thoroughness and realism that are applied in
a private-sector restructuring.

To assure that there will be at least some kind of livable
society for my grandchildren and yours, the government must
draw up a budget and say: We are going to live within our
means. It is going to hurt like hell for a while, but we are going
to do it. Furthermore, we're going to have some cash flow, and
we are going to apply it to that obscene debt. We are going to
amortize that burden over a period of years, and at some future
date a generation will be able to step forth and set an agenda of
its own instead of paying for a failed agenda of the past.

The solution itself, I fully realize, will cause its own share
of upheaval. What do you suppose happens when *any* entity
returns to reality and to the present? When Ajax Tool & Die
shuts a plant, we are talking about a much smaller universe;
but within that universe there is *total* upheaval. It is no small
consideration in restructuring the government that the nation's
Ajax Tool & Dies will have a better shot at survival.

The economists can step to the podium and crunch the theory in a thousand directions, but it seems perfectly clear to me
that when you reduce the cost of government, the money saved
will not evaporate and it will not sit idly in the pockets of the
idle rich. The tradesman who sees, through a teary eye, American jobs going to Mexico or Southeast Asia must remember that
not only is the cost of labor reduced in those locales, but so is the
cost of government.

Nonetheless, it is true that a global economy, a soaring population and dwindling resources mean that our precious American standard of living is downsizing. That is reality, and it is upon us. Restructuring our government, remember, is only a precursor to restructuring our society. We cannot have it all. We cannot work eight hours a day in a factory and maintain a second home in the woods, along with a motor home to get us there. We have to rethink that entire definition of "the American dream," because it is going to change—is in the process of changing—with or without our assent. The kids are in the basement already, and the monthly motor home payments are becoming impossible to meet.

Even as we chop away at expenses and get them within the range of reality, new expenses will be recognized—and, just like the family gathered around the table, we will have to chop some more to make room. The longstanding debate over "America's crumbling infrastructure," for example, has taken place in the absence of one vital component: money to replace the bridges and roads that we see rotting every day on the way to work. Perhaps some of the people displaced by restructuring, and some of the people already displaced by the impotent Living in the Future economy, can be put to work repairing that infrastructure. Scores of such huge decisions, and thousands of smaller ones, must be made.

Am I willing, as an affluent taxpayer, to shoulder my share of the burden? Absolutely. Knowing that I was shouldering a realistic and non-debilitative burden, in fact, would be a near-pleasure. To know that my government was not sucking its version of the good life from the blood of my grandchildren would be a joy. Nothing would please me more than to eliminate every write-off, real or cleverly invented by the attorneys and accountants; to impose a fair and reasonable flat tax upon every corporation and every citizen who makes a living wage; and to send home, the very first of all, thousands of IRS employees.

Perhaps I am wrong about signs that Americans are beginning to view the problem through much the same lens as I, that they are weary of living under the yoke of unrealistic debt and the anxiety of peering into a heavily mortgaged future. If so, there is no hope for restructuring Washington Inc. Unless the people decide that a restructuring is what they want, the scam will continue to its inevitable conclusion.

Our government has been childishly courting the Blonde Goddess, with a fervor that even I could not have imagined that summer so many years ago when I learned what it means to be insolvent. My simple solution is to put an end to the courtship. Uncle Sam must grow up. If he wants to take the Blonde Goddess to the show, it must be on a cash basis only.

As it now stands, children born for years to come will spend their summers pushing lawn mowers for nothing. I shudder to think what they, quite rightfully, will think of us all.

30

Like an Arrow into the Sky

When our daughter graduated from high school, Joan and I had a special cake created for her party. Etched in the sweet icing was an archer aiming skyward, and a quote from Kahlil Gibran's *The Prophet*.

There is more room on the page of a book than on the top of a layer cake, so let me include a longer part of the quotation here. A woman clutching an infant to her breast asks the prophet to speak of children, and he says (the italics are mine):

"Your children are not your children. They are the sons and daughters of life's longing for itself. They come through you but not from you. And though they are with you yet they belong not to you. You may give them your love but not your thoughts, for they have their own thoughts. You may house their bodies but not their souls, *for their souls dwell in the house of tomorrow, which you cannot visit—even in your dreams.*"

"For life goes not backwards nor tarries with yesterday. You are the bows from which your children as living arrows are set forth."

I am not one of the world's most well-read people. As a high-school graduate, as an old Great Lakes sailor, as an old repo man, as a man driven to build a career and invent a profession—and to extricate my family from a serious case of Living in the Future (and, having done so, to keep us in the present)—it wasn't in the cards for me to be a scholar. It is to Joan that I owe exposure to many of the gifts of reading that have enriched my life. She passed *The Prophet* on to me, as well as many other books that got my mind away from the briefcase full of balance sheets and reports that accompany me almost everywhere.

It is not unusual, I think, that I am not a great reader. It has little to do with my education and much to do with the rat race. Every day I meet professional people with several degrees hanging on their walls who may not have read anything in a month except to scan the *Wall Street Journal,* and to look at whichever professional journals apply to their 14-hour days.

Time, you see, is one of the many values that have disappeared in the new lifestyle, in the new standard of living. I am grateful that my life's partner encourages me to pass my eyes across something that does not deal with subordinated debentures, with national percentages of debt exceeding 90 days, or with an important new precedent in bankruptcy law. Life is so much more than what we do in our working hours. In fact, being in touch with as many additional dimensions as possible enriches whatever it is that you do. A Kahlil Gibran, and others I have met in print, helped me immensely toward a fuller understanding of what I already knew from experience: that dealing with financial crises transcends dollars and cents.

Thanks to Joan's literary hand-me-downs, I am a more fulfilled turnaround specialist. To develop your own ideas about the misery that you have seen, from repossessed dining room sets to bankrupt manufacturing companies, and then see those ideas clarified in the writings of skilled and disciplined thinkers is a rewarding experience. It's an experience available to all of us. I recommend it highly.

"...for their souls dwell in the house of tomorrow, which you cannot visit—even in your dreams."

I have spent an entire career watching people trying to dwell in the house of tomorrow, trying to spin reality out of dreams—something The Prophet obviously understands.

Before reading Gibran I was a sailor, an endeavor in which I heard wisdom in more profane language. In somewhat saltier terms, I learned: "You made your bunk, now sleep on it." None of the misery and pain of Living in the Future would bother me so much—certainly would not lead me to write a book—were it not for the fact that innocent children yet to be born will have to sleep on a heavily mortgaged bunk they did not make. If it is wrong to try to give our children our thoughts, what a great sin it must be to give them our debts.

Let us shoot our arrows to the sky unfettered. Plenty of problems await our children as their arc descends to Earth, without the added burden of our greed.

"What would you of me, Destiny? Behold the remnant of a flock that once filled these valleys; the remnant of your coveting. Are you come, then, to demand even more? These are the pastures your treading has rendered barren; once they were the source of sustenance and fertility. My lambs fed of the flower-tops and gave forth sweet milk. Now are their bellies empty and they gnaw thistles and tree roots out of fear that they might perish."

—A Tear and a Smile,
Kahlil Gibran

Acknowledgments

I have felt for a long time that, one day, I would write a book about what I have seen. I didn't always realize that I would be able to sum it up while sitting—as I am today, Memorial Day 1992—in our second home in Maine overlooking beautiful Boothbay Harbor.

It seems that our many friends in the Boothbay region lead a more peaceful existence. After living with them as a part-time resident for more than 20 years, I realize that this sense of peace I feel is actually the priceless ingredient of time. The Boothbay people seem to have more time than others: time for sitting, time for fishing, time for band concerts on the library lawn. Time for parades, time for singing, and just simply time to enjoy life. Life as it unfolds daily, with the many trials and beauty that it offers each of us who is content to live for whatever today may offer, rather than constantly Living in the Future—in a world that is not ours.

If you looked up front, you know that this book is dedicated to Joan. Of course. For 35 years she has been my light in a sometimes dark world. In our early married years—as my career forced us to relocate, several times—it was her willingness to travel with me, and to endure many nights of loneliness with four small children, that allowed me to accept the opportunities that God saw fit to enlighten me to recognize.

As a matter of fact, it was Joan who found Boothbay Harbor and our home at the Oak Grove in West Harbor, our Shangri-La, place of contentment, where we go—not often enough—to escape the super-stressful world of financial chaos and collapse that is central to my business.

This book is but one of so many things that would not be, except for Joni.

I also extend deep appreciation and love, as well as acknowledgement, to Scotty, who said I should; to Fred Marx, who said I could, and to my editor, Tom Ferguson, who pulled it all together and made it come true.

But most of all, to my children—Anita, Michael, Jim and John—for inspiring me, finally, that this book needed to be written. It is, in truth, written for them, and for all the other children of this generation whose lives we have unnecessarily burdened by Living in the Future.

James V. McTevia
May 25, 1992